Standards-Based Instruction and Assessment for English Language Learners

Standards-Based Instruction and Assessment for English Language Learners

MARY ANN LACHAT

CORWIN PRESS
A Sage Publications Company
Thousand Oaks, California

For information:

Corwin Press
A Sage Publications Company
2455 Teller Road
Thousand Oaks, California 91320
www.corwinpress.com

Sage Publications Ltd
1 Oliver's Yard
55 City Road
London EC1Y 1SP
United Kingdom

Sage Publications India Pvt. Ltd.
B-42, Panchsheel Enclave
Post Box 4109
New Delhi 110 017 India

Printed in the United States of America

Library of Congress Cataloging-in-Publication Data

Lachat, Mary Ann.
Standards-based instruction and assessment for English language learners/Mary Ann Lachat.
  p. cm.
Includes bibliographical references and index.
ISBN 0-7619-3892-3 (cloth) — ISBN 0-7619-3893-1 (paper)
  1. Limited English proficient students—Education—United States.
2. Education—Standards—United States. 3. Educational tests and measurements—United States. I. Title.
LC3731.L33 2004
379.1'58—dc22   2003025426

This book is printed on acid-free paper.

04   05   06   07   08   10   9   8   7   6   5   4   3   2   1

Acquisitions editor:	Rachel Livsey
Editorial assistant:	Phyllis Cappello
Production editor:	Sanford Robinson
Copy editor:	Sally M. Scott
Typesetter:	C&M Digitals (P) Ltd.
Cover designer:	Michael Dubowe

Contents

109|50

Preface

S *tandards-Based Instruction and Assessment for English Language Learners* was written to promote greater understanding of the significant issues that must be addressed to ensure a high quality education for students from diverse cultural and linguistic backgrounds. Its purpose is to translate the most important findings from the research literature into policy and practice implications that will be useful to teachers; principals; superintendents; school district personnel responsible for assessment; bilingual, ESL, and Title I program directors; and state education leaders.

Today's education reform initiatives emphasize that *all* students must be held to the same standards for learning, and they must have access to the quality of education necessary to achieve the standards. At the heart of the standards movement is an unprecedented commitment to educate *all* of the nation's children to be effective thinkers, problem solvers, and communicators so they can participate as members of the global community. At the same time, America's classrooms are becoming increasingly diverse, and students whose first language is not English are the fastest-growing school population. Known as English language learners (ELLs), these children come from very different backgrounds, and they face a considerable challenge in having to respond to the academic demands of school at the same time that they are working toward English proficiency.

Assessment and instructional practices in American schools were neither created nor designed to be responsive to the range of diversity represented in today's ELL population, but current reforms in instruction and assessment are being viewed hopefully as offering more effective strategies for educating English language learners. Nevertheless, of equal concern is that insufficient attention has been given to the cultural and linguistic factors that have an impact on instruction and assessment.

This book presents a comprehensive overview of the hopes and concerns of standards-based instruction and assessment for ELLs and their implications for school policies and practices. Chapter 1 discusses the effects of standards on educational equity and accountability, and the changes in practice that are associated with the emerging culture of standards-based assessment. Key topics in Chapter 2 include population trends and the characteristics of English language learners in America's schools, how language and culture affect learning, and language development issues for ELLs. Chapter 3 discusses a wide range of assessment issues for ELLs, and Chapter 4 provides an in-depth overview of standards-based learning practices for ELLs. The final chapter contains a set of policy and practice recommendations that support a high quality education for English language learners. The three resources provide additional self-assessment surveys and other tools for planning and developing programs and for assessing a school's policies and practices against the indicators of a high-performing school.

School and classroom practices must be consistent with our hopes for children and our vision of achieving both excellence and equity in our education system. Implementing sounder practices for English language learners will require teachers and administrators to make different decisions about instruction and assessment, develop greater awareness of how cultural and linguistic factors impact on learning, and embrace the belief that children from highly diverse backgrounds can learn at high levels. The findings of the researchers whose work is reflected here provide important perspectives that can support the work of teachers and administrators.

Acknowledgments

T he contributions of the following reviewers are gratefully acknowledged:

Dr. Roberta E. Glaser
Teacher
St. Johns Public Schools
St. Johns, MI

Dr. Maria E. Stallions
Assistant Professor of Education
Barry University
Miami Shores, FL

Dr. Margo Gottlieb
Director, Assessment and Evaluation
Illinois Resource Center
Des Plaines, IL

Dr. Sharon Toomey Clark
Educational Consultant
Clark & Associates
Claremont, CA

About the Author

Dr. Mary Ann Lachat is Co-founder and President of the Center for Resource Management, Inc. (CRM), a professional-services firm dedicated to helping schools achieve equity and high quality learning for all students. She has more than 30 years of experience with school reform initiatives at state and local levels, and she has worked extensively with state education agencies and school district teams in addressing issues for diverse learners. Since the late 1990s she has written and presented on standards-based learning and assessment for English language learners. Her work has focused on translating what has been learned in the research into practical strategies and guidelines for teachers, principals, and school district administrators. Her publications for the Northeast and Islands Regional Educational Laboratory at Brown University include: *Standards, Equity, and Cultural Diversity* (1999) and *What Policymakers and School Administrators Need to Know About Assessment Reform* (1999).

CHAPTER ONE

Achieving Equity Through Standards and Assessments

PREPARING ALL STUDENTS FOR SUCCESS

Holding all students to high academic standards is the centerpiece of a national agenda to improve schools and ensure that no child is left behind in the journey toward the American dream. The evolution of standards over the past decade has been driven by the need to define what all students should learn in school in order to participate success-fully in the twenty-first century. It has also been driven by widespread recognition that today's world requires many skills that are not being taught in schools. The issue is not whether schools are better or worse than they used to be, but whether public schools are preparing all children to succeed in today's world. Today's workplace already requires that individuals understand multidimensional problems, design solutions, plan their own tasks, evaluate results, and work cooperatively with others. These requirements demand that

American students learn a new set of competencies and foundation skills, and they demand an approach to education that is very different from the education system that served the industrial age (Lachat, 1994).

Many studies and reports have concluded that unless educational performance in the United States improves dramatically, American workers will not be able to use the technologies that will create most of the world's jobs and economic growth in the twenty-first century. The impetus for educational reform has been driven by other sources as well: cognitive research on the processes of learning; recognition of the disparities in educational opportunity for diverse student groups; concerns about the quality of the teaching force; and criticisms of the bureaucratic and departmentalized nature of the education system (Berman et al., 1995).

Historically, the standards movement reflected the belief that it is in the national interest to educate all students to their full potential. This belief became law in 1994 when Congress legislated changes in the Elementary and Secondary Education Act (ESEA), which raised the bar of achievement for every American student. This federal legislation required states to replace minimum standards for poor and academically disadvantaged students with challenging standards for all students, to develop new accountability systems aligned with the state standards, and to hold all students to the same performance standards (Riddle, 1999). The act was strengthened by the 2001 No Child Left Behind (NCLB) legislation, which defined stronger accountability mandates and is providing added momentum to the emphasis on higher standards for all students. Standards are thus the core of a federally mandated accountability system directly aimed at improving the quality of teaching and learning in American schools. The belief at the federal level is that American education will significantly change for the better if it sets high standards and uses standards-based assessments to hold districts, schools, and teachers accountable for student learning. Touching on every aspect of the education system, reform mandates are challenging long-held assumptions about how education should be conducted, particularly for students who have had the least access to high quality learning environments. The expectation is that schools will educate *all* children to be effective thinkers, problem solvers, and communicators.

The Standards Model

The standards model is based on several important assumptions: that educators can define standards for what is most important for students to know and be able to do in today's society; that most students will be able to achieve the standards; that student performance may differ in demonstrating proficiency but will still reflect the defined standards; and that standards will allow for fair and consistent assessment of diverse student performances (Taylor, 1994). Two types of standards provide the foundation for standards-based curriculum, instruction, and assessment: content standards and performance standards.

Content Standards: These standards define what children should know and be able to do. They describe the essential knowledge, skills, and understandings necessary to attain proficiency in a content area. Content standards define the focus of curriculum and instruction within and across content areas, and they describe what teachers are expected to teach and what students are expected to learn. They represent the curricular priorities of the state or district, and they can serve as starting points for curriculum improvement because they describe what is important for all students to learn in the various subject areas. *Benchmarks* are subcomponents of content standards—they identify the expected understandings and skills for a content standard at different grade levels.

Performance Standards: These standards identify levels of performance for the knowledge, skills, and understandings defined in the content standards. They set specific expectations for various levels of proficiency and provide explicit definitions and concrete examples of what students must demonstrate in order to be considered proficient in the knowledge and skills of the content standards. The emphasis is on the types of evidence that will verify the degree of proficiency the student has demonstrated. Performance standards are defined in terms of various levels of proficiency.

The standards movement has challenged educators to no longer accept low expectations for so many students. By creating stronger connections between what and how students learn in school and how they will be expected to perform in adult life, the standards movement demands instructional approaches that develop students' reasoning and problem-solving skills. This new vision of teaching and learning requires educators and the public to understand that high standards are as important in education as they are in the medical profession, in licensing pilots, or in international sports competitions such as the Olympics. They define what is essential for successful performance and encourage people to strive for the best.

Across the country, state education agencies have been implementing the standards model to power a nationwide curriculum reform movement. As of the fall of 2003, all 50 states plus the District of Columbia and Puerto Rico had completed and implemented K–12 content standards in the core subjects of English/language arts and mathematics, and 48 states had completed and implemented standards for science and social studies/history. The intent of the state content standards is that their use will help administrators, teachers, and parents develop common understandings about what students should learn.

Developing high quality education standards is a complex process, however, as was shown by the national efforts to develop content standards during the 1990s. Likewise, the process of standards development at the state level has highlighted that not all standards are equal, and the quality of state standards has come under critical review by different organizations (American Federation of Teachers, 1999; Council for Basic Education, 1998; Finn & Petrelli, 2000). Although the different organizations conducting the reviews gave very different ratings of the standards, the consensus was that state standards have improved over the past few years in the extent to which they are specific and measurable; in most states, however, they still need to be improved (Kendall & Marzano, 2000).

STANDARDS AND EDUCATIONAL EQUITY

The most pressing issue of education reform in the twenty-first century is how to ensure a high quality education for all of the nation's children, an issue that is growing in proportion to the rapidly changing demographics of America's schools. The focus on standards in federal and state mandates has shifted the emphasis from "access for all" to "high quality learning for all." Beneath the surface of standards-based reform is the question of whether the American dream truly belongs to all students and whether American society is morally committed to equal educational opportunity. In her study of the development of standards in America from the mid-1980s to the mid-1990s, Ravitch (1995) highlighted that standards-based educational reform reflected a unique convergence of people committed to excellence and people committed to quality. Her point was that people who worried most about excellence looked to standards to raise achievement; people who worried most about equality looked to standards to provide students with equal access to challenging curricula and learning experiences. Together they forged an unusual and effective alliance. From an equity perspective, the emphasis on high standards for all students springs from a vision of society where people of different backgrounds, cultures, and perceived abilities have equal access to a high quality education.

The standards movement reflects many dimensions of a new society that has emerged over the past two decades, creating totally new equity demands for schools. We are seeing an unprecedented commitment to educate *all* students to be effective thinkers, problem solvers, and communicators so they can participate as productive members of the global community. As waves of immigration bring people from all over the world to our nation, we are becoming the most ethnically, culturally, and linguistically diverse society that has ever existed. In combination, these conditions and commitments are creating a new order for schools. Never before have schools been asked to ensure that all students achieve publicly defined standards of learning. Never before have we asked schools to consider higher-order skills as core skills to be acquired by all students. Never before have teachers been faced with such diversity (Lachat, 1999a).

Historically, our education system was organized to develop basic skills for all students and higher-order proficiencies for those who were college bound. The current reform agenda disclaims this two-tier system and challenges schools to demonstrate a core belief of public education in America— that all children can learn at high levels, given the time, tools, teaching, and encouragement to do so. However, this shift in thinking is coming at a time when schools are faced with more diversity in student populations than they have ever experienced. As standards become the foundation for curriculum and instruction, many school administrators and teachers are uncertain about how to use those standards with diverse populations. Some of the questions focus on equity issues and how the same high standards can be used for all students, while other questions focus on their use with students who have not developed full proficiency in English. Nevertheless, what the standards movement will accomplish for culturally diverse students is to leave no doubt that schools must engage these students in higher-order instruction.

Evidence is growing that the use of public standards as the basis for school accountability has already motivated school administrators to avoid tracking into limiting groups those students who are not fully proficient in English, and to determine how these students can develop essential knowledge and skills. Given today's increasingly diverse student populations, the question is no longer whether it is feasible to provide a high quality education for students who vary widely in their characteristics, learning styles, levels of English proficiency, and educational needs. The question is how to reform curriculum and instruction and improve teachers' abilities to respond to diversity so that high quality learning becomes the norm for all students.

Equity and Opportunity to Learn

From an equity perspective, setting high standards for all students means that we must believe that the quality of education offered to "the best and the brightest" should be the quality of education available to all. "Watered down" curricula that deny students adequate preparation for success in an increasingly demanding world are unacceptable, and opportunity to learn has taken on a new meaning in terms of the curricular offerings and instructional methods that should be available to all students. But whether education reforms prove helpful to student populations that have been denied access to a challenging, high quality education will depend on whether these students gain access to the essential resources and conditions that support learning and achievement. Education standards and accountability mandates will not improve student learning unless they are accompanied by policies and practices that directly address inequities in conditions for learning. Curriculum reform and professional development for teachers are not enough to close achievement gaps for students who attend schools located in high-poverty environments. A vast number of students simply do not have equal access to the quality of education necessary to achieve high standards of learning.

The problem with assuming education standards will improve teaching practices for poor and language minority groups is that this assumption ignores the grossly inadequate conditions that exist in the schools they attend (Darling-Hammond, 1997; Winfield, 1995). Many of these students are in schools that receive inadequate funding, have inadequate instructional materials and technology resources, and have difficulty recruiting qualified teachers. Students in these schools have minimal opportunities to develop the proficiencies reflected in emerging standards and new assessments. At the classroom level, their opportunity to learn is influenced by curriculum content, teacher beliefs, the quality of instruction, time spent on academic tasks, the nature of teacher-student interactions, and the feedback and incentives provided to them (Neill, 1995). In addition, family support, school safety, and school climate also influence the learning of these students.

Gordon (1992) has long cautioned that education reform should not occur in a vacuum but must consider the complex societal conditions that control access to essential resources:

> [T]here are those of us who are sympathetic to standards and assessment, but insist that it is immoral to begin by measuring outcomes before we have seriously engaged the equitable and sufficient distribution of inputs, that is, opportunities and resources essential to the development of intellect and competence. (p. 2)

Widespread concerns exist about equity in the availability of school resources essential to implementing standards-based reform. Several components of organizational capacity have been identified:

- School administrators must provide the organizational leadership to implement the multiple elements of education reform.

- Schools must have certified and qualified personnel.
- Teachers must have the knowledge, skills, and capabilities to provide high quality instruction to diverse student populations.
- Financial and programmatic resources that include the high quality instructional materials, laboratories, libraries, computer facilities, and technology needed to support standards-based learning must be available.
- Teachers and administrators must have access to high quality professional development.
- The school environment must be safe and secure.
- Schools must have data system and reporting capabilities to respond to local, state, and federal requirements to demonstrate progress and accountability. (Corcoran & Goertz, 1995; Darling-Hammond, 1997; Lachat, 1999b; Newmann, King, & Rigdon, 1997; Ruiz de Velasco & Fix, 2000)

If all students are to have an equal opportunity to learn the knowledge and skills essential to success, inequities in how educational resources are allocated must be eliminated. The school capacity (i.e., a school's ability to respond to multiple demands) and resource implications of "high standards for all students" have yet to be fully determined, particularly for schools that serve poor and linguistically diverse student populations. But the mandates driving standards-based education reform can provide the much-needed leverage for addressing equity issues—the leverage to ensure all schools and teachers are aiming at the same high goals; the leverage to reduce inequities in the resources available to schools; and the leverage to ensure all students have equal access to instructional environments that support learning and achievement. Organizing school curricula around clearly defined standards may put an end to the inferior education that now deprives many children of the chance to study a challenging curriculum. However, the success of standards-based reform is directly connected to a comprehensive set of changes involving access to resources, access to highly skilled teachers, access to high quality instruction, and a safe and supportive school environment.

THE CULTURE OF STANDARDS-BASED ASSESSMENT

States have adopted the standards model to develop the assessment systems that will be used to measure the progress of all students. These emerging systems represent a different way of thinking about large-scale assessment, and they are playing a central role in school reform. For the first time, student learning is being measured against publicly defined standards, and performance-based assessment methods are being used to measure student proficiencies. These assessments focus on improving student learning and as a result are creating new concepts of accountability for schools. Standards-based assessments have several important features:

- They focus attention on what is most important to learn.
- They compare students to a standard of proficiency, not to other students.
- They are linked to curriculum and instruction.
- They are intended to establish accountability, as well as stimulate improvement.

Standards-based assessments represent a profound and sweeping shift away from the beliefs of a testing culture to the beliefs of an assessment culture, and they reflect changing assumptions about the nature of intelligence and how people learn. Testing and assessment cultures have radically different belief systems and goals. Helping educators and the public understand the implications of this change in belief systems is one of the challenges of education reform.

The Traditional Testing Culture

Traditional testing practices in America did not match the vision of standards-based reform. Historically, standardized tests had not been designed to measure complex skills and performance abilities and, as a result, often drove instruction toward lower-order cognitive skills (Darling-Hammond, 1997; Linn, 2000). Therefore, testing practices often contributed to the educational problems plaguing many schools. Based on a measurement model, the testing culture that dominated American education for most of the twentieth century assumed that intelligence and learning capacity were fixed traits that could be predicted. Because of this assumption, educators believed that students had an inherent level of intelligence that governed what they were able to learn. Therefore, the aim of testing was to rank students for purposes of comparison and placement. Testing was traditionally used to sort students according to their abilities (presumed to be inherent) and then to track them into "appropriate" educational programs (Taylor, 1994). Testing practices thus served to limit the access that some students had to higher-level learning opportunities, and students from low-income and varied cultural and language backgrounds particularly experienced the negative impacts of testing policies.

The impact of ranking on American education was far reaching. Founded on early-twentieth-century theories that treated intelligence as a unitary, fixed trait, America's testing culture encouraged the belief that individuals could be ranked according to mental capacities. Scores representing children's abilities were positioned relative to one another on a normal curve, causing educators to confuse a student's rank with his or her potential for success (Wolf, Bixby, Glenn, & Gardner, 1991). The use of the normal curve as the dominant profile for showing student achievement led to widespread acceptance among policymakers, administrators, and teachers that a significant percentage of students would fail. Therefore, the belief system of the testing culture provided the public school system with a scientific rationale for tracking, and schools were not held accountable for the learning and academic success of all students. In short, the quality of education made available to many students was undermined by the testing policies and practices used to define and monitor their learning, and they were denied the opportunity to develop the capacities they needed to succeed.

The testing culture also did not emphasize complex and rich ways of demonstrating learning. Focusing on a narrow range of cognitive abilities that magnified differences among students, the testing culture valued accuracy, speed, and easily quantifiable skills. The selection of test items, which ranged from very easy to very difficult, was based on how well items discriminated between high and low scores so that scores could be easily differentiated and ranked (Farr & Trumbull, 1997). High proportions of those students who received low scores were poor students and students learning English as a second language. Because of their low test scores, these students were placed in low-level classes. Until the mid-1990s, testing was predominantly used to group these students according to levels of ability and provided a long-standing excuse for the limited learning opportunities that were provided to so many students.

Today's Assessment Culture

The focus on high standards for all students that began in the 1990s also caused a re-evaluation of the purpose of assessment by shifting the emphasis away from ranking students against test norms to an emphasis on improving student learning. This shift in emphasis was closely tied to the recognition that traditional testing practices had fueled inequities in education by relegating many students to a low-level education that limited their learning opportunities and life choices. The emerging assessment culture uses assessment as a tool to help schools understand their students' proficiencies against publicly defined learning standards. The use of assessment has therefore changed from deciding which students will have access to a high quality education to determining whether all students are learning at high levels. Under this form of assessment, students are compared to a standard of performance, not to other students. At the policy level, this shift is significant. When students are measured against publicly defined standards of achievement, rather than against national norms established by test companies, more open discussion of the appropriateness of the assessment standards is possible. If the conception, development, and interpretation of assessment become open processes, then hidden biases can become more visible and more of the public will have a clear sense of what counts in our schools (Garcia & Pearson, 1994).

New forms of assessment are based on cognitive research that created new understandings about how children learn. The research challenged outmoded theories of learning that fostered the testing of sequential rote instruction but not critical thinking. It created a new vision of assessment that was developmental, went beyond a narrow range of skills, and offered new ways of examining how students think and perform when solving complex problems. Underlying the new approach is the belief that intelligence is not a fixed trait; instead, learning potential is considered to be developmental and a function of experience. An assessment culture recognizes that intelligence is multifaceted— that people's multiple intelligences have varying degrees of strength, are at various stages of development, and thus cannot be accurately ranked according to a single dimension (Gardner, 1993).

By shifting from a "measurement model" to a "standards model," assessment now focuses on how student performance develops relative to standards of excellence, not on how each student ranks against other students. This profoundly changes the playing field for students who are not yet fully proficient in English and who must have access to educational opportunities that foster development learning. The onus is now on the schools to provide these opportunities rather than sorting students into limited opportunities. A summary of the differences between the current assessment culture and the testing culture that dominated American education for most of the twentieth century is shown in Figure 1.1.

Figure 1.1   Comparison of a testing culture and an assessment culture

The Testing Culture	The Assessment Culture
Views intelligence as a unitary, fixed trait.	Views intelligence as multifaceted and learning potential as developmental.
Based on a measurement model that treats students' abilities as relative positions on a normal curve.	Based on a standards model where achievement is criterion-referenced.
Emphasizes accuracy, speed, and easily quantifiable skills.	Focuses on what students can do (performance), not just what they know (content domain).
Focuses on a narrow range of cognitive abilities.	Emphasizes complex and rich ways of demonstrating learning.
Views testing and instruction as separate activities.	Regards assessment as central to instruction.
Determines how students rank and compare with each other.	Determines how students perform relative to standards of excellence.
Uses test results to sort students into classes and courses emphasizing differential abilities.	Uses assessment results to improve teaching and learning.

The Use of Performance Assessments

When assessments are tied to standards, students must demonstrate what they know and can do through a range of "performances," and more emphasis is placed on tasks that involve higher-order thinking and more complex problem solving. Performance assessments offer a better way of measuring the attainment of high learning standards than do traditional assessments. Wiggins (1989) was an early proponent of performance assessment as a more appropriate and meaningful way to assess student learning, suggesting that student performances that were "authentic" to the concepts, knowledge, and skills of a discipline and based on real-world problems could be identified for all subject areas. When he first recommended that these identified performances should form the foundation of new assessment programs, his writings provoked strong response from policymakers and educators. At the time, although many educators were dissatisfied with standardized achievement tests, they also saw traditional tests as the only way to ensure fair and reliable large-scale testing.

Today, however, performance-based assessment is rapidly becoming accepted as a promising vehicle for state assessment programs that are showing an increased emphasis on performance approaches. Most of the states are using some form of performance assessment in their assessment programs, particularly for the content areas of writing, mathematics, and reading. The challenge of large-scale assessment is that performance assessments rely on the judgment of those scoring the tests. The assessor must apply clearly articulated performance criteria in making a professional judgment about the level of proficiency demonstrated. The scoring process has to look beyond right or wrong answers; it also has to consider the thoughtfulness of the procedures used to carry out the task or solve the problem (Baker, 1997).

New Criteria for Validity and Reliability

The emergence of standards-based state assessment systems has forced experts who deal with the technical aspects of assessment to rethink their methods for assuring quality. The litmus test for any measuring instrument has always been its degrees of reliability (the degree to which the test yields the same results on repeated trials) and validity (the degree to which a test measures what it is intended to measure and to which inferences made based on a test's results are appropriate and useful for all students). In the past, test development often sacrificed validity to achieve reliability, in effect sacrificing the students' interests to the interests of test developers (Baker & Linn, 2002). However, new approaches to assessment have led some to question the role that reliability has traditionally played in assessment. Content validity, or the ability to understand what student performance reveals about learning, is of primary importance in standards-based assessment. Because of this, the traditional emphasis on reliability is being re-examined.

By their nature, performance assessments often require integrated knowledge and skills; are far less standardized than traditional tests; and allow for more latitude in design, in student response, and in scorer interpretation. Because of this, establishing reliability has been a major issue in new state assessment systems. Establishing consistency in scoring among well-trained raters has been more successful than establishing consistency across tasks. For example, test developers have had difficulty in establishing acceptable levels of comparability (reliability) across tasks intended to address the same skills. Some research shows that consistency of performance across tasks is influenced by the extent to which tasks share comparable features and also reflect the types of instruction students had received. Research also has shown that variations in task performance may be attributable to differences in students' prior knowledge and their experiences in performing similar tasks (Pellegrino, Chudowsky, & Glaser, 2001). This has significant implications for students who are not from the mainstream culture and who are not fully proficient in English.

Researchers have given increasing attention to the validity criteria that should characterize the use of performance assessments in large-scale statewide assessment programs (Baker & Linn, 2002). Leading assessment specialists recommend that these assessments exemplify current content standards for what students should know and be able to do in various subject areas, and they should also contain explicit standards for rating or judging performance. The assessments should require that complex cognition be demonstrated through knowledge representation and problem solving. The validity criteria recommended by assessment specialists also stress that performance assessments be fair to students of different backgrounds and meaningful to students and teachers, incorporating competencies that can be taught and learned.

The emergence of large-scale performance assessments has therefore highlighted the importance of establishing a connection between validity standards and the interpretation and use of assessment results for diverse student populations. Due to the growing intolerance of test policies that limit students' access to learning, the concept of *consequential validity* has emerged. Consequential validity stresses that an assessment's *use* is what matters—that is, whether the use of assessment results produces positive consequences for students and for the teaching and learning process (Farr & Trumbull, 1997). It draws attention to the inequities produced when test results are used to limit educational opportunities. Consequential validity emphasizes that the use of assessment results is as important as technical concerns about reliability and content validity, and that tests must be evaluated in terms of their effects on the lives of students.

Accountability and Equity

The premise of high standards for all students is the greatest accountability challenge of the standards movement, particularly in low-performing schools with high proportions of culturally and linguistically diverse students. For the first time, schools are expected to ensure that *all* students achieve publicly defined standards of learning. For the first time, schools must consider "higher-order" skills as *core* skills to be acquired by all students, not just the most gifted. This represents a new way of thinking, a paradigm shift calling for high expectations for every student in every school, not just some students in some schools. This shift represents a very different mission for schools and a new emphasis on accountability for the success of all students.

Because standards-based assessments are part of the push toward higher levels of learning, they drive demands that schools verify that all students, including students who are not fully proficient in English, are achieving at acceptable levels. When policymakers link higher standards of performance to school accountability, however, they provoke considerable discussion and debate. To many educators, the drive for accountability exemplifies the kind of top-down approach to educational change that undermines reflective practices in teaching and learning. Other educators see accountability as a necessary part of current efforts to reform schools. At the heart of the debate is the widespread recognition that, even if external authorities establish higher standards and provide inducements, many schools will still lack the organizational capacity to get their students to achieve at high levels (Newmann et al., 1997). As noted previously, many schools lack the necessary resources to respond to the needs of increasingly diverse student populations. Therefore, when schools are held accountable for ensuring that all students achieve high standards of learning, many complex issues are raised about the inequities that exist among schools.

Widespread concerns also exist about the use of penalties to enforce accountability when standards-based assessment systems are used. Accountability is an essential stimulus in achieving the scope of change needed in schools, but it is far more complex to implement than it is possible to define in typical state mandates. While schools owe their constituencies honest accounts of what they have and have not achieved, narrow visions of accountability can result in assessment being driven too exclusively by concerns for reporting achievement data to external audiences. In the early stages of the current accountability in education, Wolf, LeMahieu, and Eresch (1992) emphasized the importance of internal accountability—encouraging students, teachers, and families to reflect on what is worth knowing, and ensuring that all students have the opportunity to develop essential knowledge. Internal accountability thus becomes as important as external mandates in addressing equity and excellence in the learning opportunities provided to students.

C H A P T E R   T W O

Understanding Today's English Language Learners

The national mandate for high learning standards in America's schools has great potential for improving the quality of education offered to students whose first language is not English. Known as English language learners (ELLs), this population includes both students who are just beginning to learn English and those who have already developed considerable proficiency. The term "English language learner" is a recent designation reflecting a positive focus on what these students are accomplishing—mastering another language. Educators, researchers, and advocates of this population prefer this term to "limited English proficient" (LEP), the designation used in federal and state education legislation and most national and state data collection efforts (August & Hakuta, 1997).

WHO ARE AMERICA'S ENGLISH LANGUAGE LEARNERS?

English language learners are the fastest-growing population group in public schools today. Their growing numbers reflect demographic trends occurring over the past 20 years that are changing the make-up of communities across the United States. This growing diversity reflects the fact that one in five children under eight years of age in America is the child of an immigrant, a statistic that has tripled over the past few decades and will continue to grow. By the turn of the twenty-first century, census figures indicated that more than half of the children in New York City and more than 60% of the children in Los Angeles were children of immigrants (Ruiz de Velasco & Fix, 2000). The changing face of America is also changing the definition of "diversity" itself to encompass more than the common determinants of race and ethnicity; it now also includes the cultural and socioeconomic factors that affect how a person is viewed by and interacts with society (Trail, 2000). The 2000 census reflected the blurring of "race" classifications by allowing people to check more than one race on the form; as a result, people of mixed heritages did not have to choose a single classification.

English language learners are a cross-section of the public-school student population, and any description of them as a whole is a generalization that can mask character-istics that are important to understanding their educational needs. There is no typical English language learner. About 55% are native born and 45% are foreign born. Meeting their instructional needs is an enormous challenge because of their cultural and linguistic diversity. Although they share the need to build proficiency in English, they differ from each other in their country of origin, language and cultural backgrounds, socioeconomic status, family histories, length of time in the United States, mobility, level of education prior to immigrating to the United States, level of parent educa-tion, and educational goals. Even within groups of immi-grants, there are considerable differences. For example, the first wave of Southeast Asian immigrants, in the early 1980s, was composed of highly educated people who could provide active home support to their child's learning and transition to a new environment. Subsequent immigrants had less education and were perhaps less able to provide such support (Kopriva, 2000). It is also important to note that a proportion of Native American students are considered English language learners, as are other groups in the United States. In other words,

> the umbrella of "English language learner" includes students from Native American communities that have been in what is now the United States from time immemorial; students from other long-established language minority communities, such as Franco-Americans in the Northeast, Latino and Chicano in the Southwest, and the Amish in the Midwest; and students from migrant and immigrant groups who represent the most recent arrivals in a virtually unbroken series of migrations that have brought linguistic diversity to North America. (LaCelle-Peterson & Rivera, 1994, p. 59)

A significant characteristic of English language learners is that a large proportion of them live in high-poverty areas and segregated neighborhoods beset with an array of problems—insufficient employment opportunities, inadequate health and social services, and crime. They attend schools with high concentrations of other poor students—schools that tend to be underfunded and poorly maintained, and staffed with large numbers of minimally prepared and unlicensed staff. Research has shown that schools with large numbers of poor students tend to emphasize the teaching of basic skills rather than higher-order skills, have limited access to technology, and offer limited or no early childhood and preschool programs. These factors increase the risk of failure for students who attend these schools. In addition, English language learners also experience the considerable discrimination that results from the prejudices of society and that some school personnel feel toward immigrants, ethnic minorities, and poor people (Berman et al., 1995).

Garcia (2000) pointedly summarized the potentially negative impact of these factors on every aspect of English language learners' education—"their readiness to learn in general; to learn English in particular; to learn grade-appropriate subject matter; to stay in school; and to go on to college and have meaningful careers. These students represent a schooling dilemma of national proportions" (p. 5).

DEFINITIONS OF ENGLISH LANGUAGE PROFICIENCY

Several terms are used to describe the language background and English language proficiency of students. The following are the most commonly used terms (Linquanti, 1999):

English only: Students who speak English as a native language and do not speak any other language.

Language minority: Students from homes where the primary language spoken is not English. These students may be limited English proficient or fluent in English as defined below.

Limited English proficient or English language learner: Students whose level of fluency in speaking, reading, writing, or understanding the English language is likely to limit their ability to succeed academically in a mainstream English classroom. The term "limited English proficient" is the federal and state designation for students whose primary language is not English. State definitions have varied. The following definition was given in the Improving America's School's Act, Title VIII, 1994, and is the term used in the current No Child Left Behind legislation.

A student who is limited English proficient includes: an individual

A. who–

1. was not born in the United States or whose native language is a language other than English and comes from an environment where a language other than English is dominant; or

2. is a Native American or who is a native resident of the outlying areas and comes from an environment where a language other than English has had a significant impact on such individual's level of English language proficiency; or

3. is migratory and whose native language is other than English and comes from an environment where a language other than English is dominant; and

B. who has sufficient difficulty speaking, reading, writing, or understanding the English language and whose difficulties may deny such individual the opportunity to learn successfully in classrooms where the language of instruction is English, or to participate fully in our society.

Fluent English proficient: Language minority students who have been assessed as able to read, comprehend, speak, and write English at a level that they can function successfully in a mainstream English classroom without special language support services or accommodations.

To provide more clarity about what "fluent English proficiency" means, an advisory committee to the Council of Chief State School Officers (CCSSO) developed the following definition of students who had developed "full English proficiency":

A *fully English proficient* student is able to use English to ask questions, to understand teachers and reading materials, to test ideas, and to challenge what is being asked in the classroom. Four language skills contribute to proficiency:

> *Reading*–the ability to comprehend and interpret text at the age- and grade-appropriate level.
>
> *Listening*–the ability to understand the language of the teacher, to comprehend and extract information, and to follow the instructional discourse through which teachers provide information.
>
> *Writing*–the ability to produce written text whose content and format fulfill classroom assignments at the age- and grade-appropriate level.
>
> *Speaking*–the ability to use oral language appropriately and effectively in learning activities within the classroom (such as peer tutoring, collaborative learning activities, and question/answer sessions) and in social interactions within the school. (Clements, Lara, & Cheung, 1992, p. 27)

In the past, it was difficult to determine accurately the number of English language learners in the nation's schools because of the inconsistency of procedures used across states, districts, and schools to identify these students. Recent surveys conducted by the U.S. Department of Education showed more consistency in the procedures used across states. Data gathered through the annual "Survey of the States' Limited English Proficient Students and Available Programs and Services" indicated a tremendous growth in the reported number of limited English proficient students enrolled in public schools between 1990–91 and 2001–02—a growth of 95% compared to an increase of 12% in the total K–12 enrollment. This growth is shown in Table 2.1 and is likely due to a combination of demographic trends and the

Table 2.1   Growing Enrollment of Limited English Proficient Students in Public Schools

Year	Total K–12 Enrollment	Growth Since 1991	LEP Enrollment	Growth Since 1991
91–92	43,134,517	—	2,430,712	—
92–93	44,444,939	3%	2,735,952	13%
93–94	45,443,389	5%	3,037,922	25%
94–95	47,745,835	11%	3,184,696	31%
95–96	47,582,665	10%	3,228,799	33%
96–97	46,714,980	8%	3,452,073	42%
97–98	46,023,969	7%	3,470,268	43%
98–99	46,153,266	7%	3,540,673	46%
99–00	47,356,089	10%	4,416,580	82%
00–01	47,665,483	11%	4,584,946	89%
01–02	48,296,777	12%	4,747,763	95%

Source: U.S. Department of Education annual "Survey of the States' Limited English Proficient Students and Available Programs and Services," 1991–1992 and 2001–2002.

use of more consistent procedures to identify LEP students in the school population.

According to the 2001–02 annual survey, the LEP public school enrollment had exceeded 4.7 million students and represented 10% of the total student population. More than 44% of these students were enrolled in PreK–3, with smaller numbers in succeeding grades—35% in Grades 4–8 and 19% at the high school level. Spanish is the native language of most LEP students (79%), followed by Vietnamese (2%), Hmong (2%), Cantonese (1%), and Korean (1%). Although Spanish is the predominant native language, state surveys indicated the broad linguistic diversity represented in the multitude of immigrant populations entering public schools; nationwide, they speak more than 460 languages and dialects. State surveys also show considerable regional variation in linguistic diversity. For example, while Spanish is the dominant language of LEP students in nine states, French is the dominant language of these students in Maine,

Hmong in Minnesota, and Serbo-Croatian in Vermont (Kindler, 2002).

WHERE IS THE GREATEST CONCENTRATION OF ENGLISH LANGUAGE LEARNERS?

With the increasing diversity of the nation's population, fewer and fewer schools have a student population of exclusively native English speakers. However, the population trends that are creating greater diversity are not distributed evenly across the nation. Nearly 80% of all English language learners are concentrated in seven states, with about 40% enrolled in California's public schools (Kindler, 2002). Nevertheless, almost every region, state, city, district, and school is experiencing continuous demographic changes, with numbers that are not stable because of the increasing trend of population mobility (Trail, 2000). In his review of the demographic trends of the millennium, Hodgkinson (2000) made the point that, with more than 30 million Americans moving every year, diversity in the classroom is more a function of migration than a function of who was born in the local community.

Rapid growth in the immigrant population has led to their movement to areas that were not the traditional gateway states and cities. This is causing major shifts in the population characteristics of states and communities that had not been traditional destinations for immigrants. With the exception of Florida (which has long had many LEP students), southern and midwestern states are showing the greatest changes in K–12 enrollment of LEP students (Kindler, 2002). Smaller school districts in these states are particularly affected by changing enrollments and struggle to meet the instructional needs of students because of limited resources and few staff with experience in educating language minority children (Ruiz de Velasco & Fix, 2000).

THE CHALLENGES FACED BY ENGLISH LANGUAGE LEARNERS

In school, the greatest difference between English language learners and their peers is the magnitude of learning expected of the former. The English language learners need to work toward English proficiency for both social and academic purposes, and they face the same academic challenges as other students. Compounding these challenges is the fact that only a small subset of English language learners who come from other countries have strong educational backgrounds (LaCelle-Peterson & Rivera, 1994). For most English language learners, achieving educational success is a daunting task. Today, two populations are of particular concern. One group is foreign-born teenagers who have limited time to master a new language and pass the subjects and/or state assessment requirements necessary for high school graduation. A subgroup of this population is underschooled middle and high school newcomers with critical literacy gaps. These students bring very weak foundation skills to the learning that is essential to their success in school. Recent reports indicate that secondary schools are experiencing major difficulties in providing these students with any of the special instructional or support services that address their specific language development needs (U.S. Department of Education, Office for Civil Rights, 1998).

HOW CULTURE AFFECTS THE LEARNING OF ENGLISH LANGUAGE LEARNERS

Many factors affect the academic performance of English language learners. Poverty and social inequities block some from achieving success, while others simply do not have sufficient access to educational resources and opportunities. Growing evidence suggests, however, that many children do poorly in school mainly because their cultural frames of reference do not match those of the mainstream American classroom. Learning is both a cultural and a social process, and students construct knowledge by relating academic content to their lives and by learning from others. Therefore, an English language learner's poor performance in school does not necessarily come from a lack of competence in school subjects; instead, difficulty in school may be caused by learning tasks that are poorly matched to the student's home culture and the cultural orientations that powerfully influence learning (August & Pease-Alvarez, 1996; Estrin & Nelson-Barber, 1995).

Differences in Ways of Knowing and Learning

How people categorize the world, organize information, and interpret their experiences differs strikingly from culture to culture.

> Cultural and linguistic diversity brings with them diversity in cognitive and communicative styles, problem-solving approaches, systems of knowledge, and methods and styles of assessment. What counts as intelligent behavior is variable from culture to culture; what counts as knowledge and evidence for knowing something, as well as appropriate ways of displaying knowledge are also culturally variable. (Farr & Trumbull, 1997, p. 15)

Each English language learner brings to the school setting a distinctive set of cultural beliefs and behavioral norms that reflect his or her cultural way of understanding the world. Because of these cultural differences in the ways they learn, children from varied backgrounds not only speak and interact differently, but they also think and learn in distinct ways (August & Pease-Alvarez, 1996). Meaningful learning occurs when school experiences connect to the ways their culture has taught them to know and understand the world.

Differences in Prior Knowledge and Experiences

Another cultural factor that impacts the learning process is the set of common experiences and understandings that students bring to learning situations. When learning tasks draw on the common experiences and language uses of students' homes and communities, the students' prior knowledge helps them understand what is expected. For students who are familiar with mainstream cultural assumptions, continuities exist between the home culture and school; for many English language learners, these continuities do not exist. Thus, schools that do not make efforts to connect learning activities to the cultural orientations and prior knowledge of English language learners place these students at an educational disadvantage. Because the home and school cultures of many English language learners do not match, their learning potential is underestimated and their strengths are ignored (Koelsch, Estrin, & Farr, 1995).

Differences in Cultural Values

How people think about the world and how people should behave in society can be very different from culture to culture. In his analysis of demographic changes in the twenty-first century, Hodgkinson (2000) highlighted important differences in how people from different cultures view *time, family,* and *hierarchy.* The American culture places a strong emphasis on future success, whereas many cultures honor the past, with historic traditions shaping how people think and act in their daily lives. The sense of an extended family is also much stronger in other cultures than in America, reflecting differences in how parents and other family members interact with children. Finally, many of today's immigrants come from more rigid and authoritative societies where, in many cases, women and children are not treated with respect. In many societies, teachers are viewed as authority figures, and active and dynamic communication between teachers and students is neither expected nor encouraged.

Implications for Classroom Teachers

The important lesson for mainstream teachers is that creating meaningful learning contexts for English language learners involves noticing how instruction and assessment connect to their cultural values, experiences, and prior knowledge. How students approach a learning task, formulate an argument, or communicate what they have learned affects how they perform and how they will be evaluated. Cultural differences affect students' understanding of the content presented in a classroom, their interactions with teachers and other students, and their behavior in a learning situation. For example, students from some cultures may think that it is disrespectful to look directly at a teacher or ask questions. Therefore, we cannot fully understand why students behave and perform as they do without an awareness of how cultural differences affect their performance (Garcia & Pearson, 1994; Zehler, 1994).

To draw on cultural contexts, a teacher must know about different cultures, be aware of the range of language uses across cultures, and understand that differences in communication and thinking styles do not mean deficiency in ability. Developing an awareness of the cultural and linguistic differences that students bring to a learning situation does not mean that teachers have to come up with different teaching strategies for each student. Cultural awareness is an avenue that helps teachers understand and appreciate the range of values, learning styles, and possibilities that students bring to the classroom (Koelsch et al., 1995). With an appreciation of the cultural contexts that students bring to the learning situation, teachers can find pertinent cultural examples, re-create classroom discourse so that what is being taught connects to what students already know, and "probe the school community, and home environments in a search for insights into students' abilities, preferences, motivations, and learning approaches" (Irvine & York, 1995, p. 494).

It is also important to recognize that classroom diversity can be an important resource for all students by providing exposure to unique and varying backgrounds, experiences, and perspectives. Zehler (1994) highlighted three ways that the diverse cultural and linguistic backgrounds of English language learners can enrich classroom teaching and learning:

- Through *information* about other countries and their cultures, customs, and resources.
- Through *new perspectives* about the world, society, and cultural belief systems.
- Through *opportunities* for students to become exposed to other languages, and to share ways of thinking and doing things that are otherwise taken for granted.

Using cultural diversity as a resource for classroom learning benefits all students. Making the connection to the life experiences of English language learners helps to make learning more real and meaningful to them, and it offers other students opportunities to learn about different cultural perspectives.

THE LANGUAGE DEVELOPMENT OF ENGLISH LANGUAGE LEARNERS

Language is both the primary medium through which people experience the world and the primary symbol system a culture uses to describe and interpret its environment and to communicate and represent its knowledge. "It is through language that we learn about the world that surrounds us—how to interact with others and objects within that world, how to think about it, how to represent ourselves within it" (Farr & Trumbull, 1997, p. 89). While a child's interactions with family and community influence his or her language use, the interaction of language and culture shape how people conceive of, demonstrate, and measure learning because cultures vary in their methods of teaching and assessing children in both informal (home and community) and formal (school) settings. As Gardner (1993) observed in outlining his theory of multiple intelligences, while all children develop symbolic competence, they learn quite different symbol systems that reflect the values, beliefs, and norms of their respective cultures. How people use language to structure learning and to show what they have learned varies from culture to culture.

Variability in Language Development

Tailoring language development programs for English language learners of different ages with a wide range of native languages, a wide range of language abilities, and very different academic backgrounds is a major challenge for schools. However, although educators are quick to recognize and accept the variability in learning styles and language development of mainstream students, they are less willing to accept that there is no fixed time frame for how long it takes English language learners to develop sufficient proficiency in English to use it for academic purposes.

Research has shown that, although there are many similarities in how a second language is learned, there are also many differences based on the language background and other characteristics of a student. In his analysis of factors that have an impact on the amount of time it takes these students to learn English, Garcia (2000) noted the wide variability in their language backgrounds and in home literacy practices. Many of them grew up speaking languages other than English at home, while others grew up mostly speaking English; still others grew up in multilingual households where English was just one of the languages spoken. Very few grew up speaking English fluently. In addition, some native-born English language learners are not proficient in English, but not in the same way as foreign-born students. For example, some speak social dialects of English that have been influenced by their ethnic backgrounds and the neighborhoods in which they live. These dialects do not match the form of English spoken in schools (August & Hakuta, 1997; Garcia, 2000; Kopriva, 2000).

Considerable research also shows that "young children do not learn a second language effortlessly, that they do not learn faster with more exposure to the new language, that their oral fluency outstrips their academic competence, and that they require many years to reach grade-level academic ability in the new language" (Berman, 1997, p. 17). Generally, older children have developed some learning strategies that help them learn a second language, and they can learn the vocabulary and grammar of a new language faster than younger children can. What is also confounding to many mainstream educators is that many English language learners who understand spoken English and speak English fluently may still have difficulty reading and writing proficiently in English (McLaughlin, 1992). "Fluency on the playground does not necessarily mean proficiency in the classroom" (Zehler, 1994, p. 4).

For more than a decade, Collier and Thomas investigated the "how long" question, and found that non-native speakers of English who had two to three years of instruction in their home language prior to immigrating to the United States took at least five to seven years to reach grade level on academic aspects of the English language (Collier, 1995). Their findings suggested that students with no formal schooling in their first language would need a longer time frame to learn English. As Garcia (2000) noted, however, the averages noted in the literature for how long it takes English language learners to develop proficiency in English "mask variability and differences in student abilities, readiness, motivation, and opportunities to become sufficiently proficient in English to succeed in mainstream classrooms" (p. 3).

A major finding of a recent national study of school effectiveness for language minority students indicated that the strongest predictor of student academic achievement in their second language was the amount of grade-level schooling in the first language (Thomas & Collier, 2002). This study reflected earlier research findings indicating that the degree of native language proficiency is a strong predictor of English language development (August & Hakuta, 1997). A considerable body of research has shown that there is no quick path to developing academic second language proficiency and then achieving academic success in the second language. The work of Collier (1987, 1995) has particularly highlighted the daunting challenge for school-age immigrants who face the demands of learning all aspects of a second language in the context of its use for academic purposes.

> Immigrants of school age who must acquire a second language in the context of schooling need to develop full proficiency in all language domains (including the structures and semantics of phonetics, phonology, inflectional morphology, syntax, vocabulary, discourse, pragmatics, and paralinguistics) and all language skills (listening, speaking, and writing), and metalinguistic knowledge of the language for use in all content areas (language arts, mathematics, science, and social studies). (Collier, 1987, p. 618)

The Politics of English Language Acquisition

A major issue in the political debate occurring in states with large concentrations of English language learners is how long English language learners should receive language support services or participate in bilingual or English as a Second Language programs. The rationale is that English language learners should be mainstreamed and immersed in English instruction as soon as possible. However, decisions are being driven not by research knowledge on language acquisition or by an understanding of the variability of the population, their characteristics, and their learning needs; instead, decisions are being driven by political sentiment about the need to become "Americanized," as did previous waves of immigrants; widespread public ignorance of the complexity of the issue; insufficient resources to provide adequate support programs for these students; and a serious lack of knowledge among mainstream educators.

SCHOOL LANGUAGE USES THAT IMPACT ON ENGLISH LANGUAGE LEARNERS

In school, the language structures used to communicate learning tasks influence how students conceptualize tasks, and they provide the vehicle for understanding and solving problems. It is no surprise, therefore, that English language learners face unique challenges when they tackle learning tasks. In the daily life of schools, three factors particularly affect the ability of English language learners to succeed academically:

- The speaking patterns used for instruction are not familiar to many English language learners, and the language used to demonstrate learning does not match the cognitive and communication patterns of many English language learners' home cultures.
- The English language facility of these students is insufficient for the language demands of many learning tasks.
- Regular classroom teachers have not received sufficient preparation and training in fundamental aspects of linguistics, language development, and second language acquisition.

Patterns of Speaking in the Classroom

In classroom learning situations, students have to understand the rules for speaking and the acceptable patterns for communicating what they know. Adopting discourse patterns that are grounded in the communication styles of the mainstream culture is much more difficult for children learning a second language (August & Hakuta, 1997). For example, as two leading researchers noted in 1994,

> Mainstream school culture has promoted a widespread discourse pattern for classroom discussions. Interactions tend to follow a pattern in which the teacher initiates an interaction, students respond, and the teacher evaluates. Teachers use this pattern for a variety of classroom discourse functions, including assessing student learning. Inferences that teachers draw from such interactions assume that students are familiar with and recognize the discourse function of the pattern. Sociolinguistic evidence does not support the validity of such an assumption. (Garcia & Pearson, 1994, p. 364)

When English language learners do not respond to the classroom speaking patterns that are unfamiliar to them, educators often mistakenly think that students' ability to learn, rather than their communication style, is the source of difficulty.

In addition, how students from varied backgrounds use language to demonstrate their learning often does not match the patterns of classroom communication. Expository styles, patterns of speaking, methods of argumentation, and even rules of good writing differ from one culture to another. For example, one typical style of language use in American schools is to present a topic in a sequential and linear way, providing evidence and then drawing conclusions. However, Asian and Native American language styles tend to be holistic and circular, presenting multiple topics that are interrelated. In some cultures it is not appropriate to ask people questions, while in other cultures students are not accustomed to being asked to respond to a timed task. It is not surprising, then, that many English language learners experience difficulties when their orientation to language use is so different from that of the school they attend (Garcia, 2000).

The Center for Applied Linguistics (1998) recommended eleven ways that teachers can adjust their speech to increase comprehension for English language learners: face the students; pause frequently; paraphrase often; clearly indicate

Figure 2.1   Strategies to promote student understanding of classroom discourse

- Restate complex sentences as a sequence of simple sentences.
- Avoid or explain the use of idiomatic expressions.
- Restate information at a slower pace.
- Pause often to allow students to process what they hear.
- Provide explanations of key words and special technical vocabulary.
- Bring in objects, photographs, or other materials to explain content.
- Use visual organizers and graphics to organize and illustrate key points.
- Provide an outline of a lesson that students can review.
- Allow time for students to discuss what they have learned and to generate questions about areas that need more clarification.

Source: Zehler, 1994.

the most important ideas and vocabulary through intonation or writing on the blackboard; avoid "asides"; avoid or clarify pronouns; use shorter sentences; use subject-verb-object word order; increase wait time to allow students to answer; focus on students' meaning, not grammar; and avoid interpreting on a regular basis.

Teachers can adapt language use and provide support in a classroom to English language learners in many different ways, so the students can gain a better understanding of what is being said and the meaning of instruction. Figure 2.1 provides a number of examples (Zehler, 1994).

Language Demands of Academic English

The language of instruction in American schools presents a major obstacle to many English language learners because of their limited language skills. The difficulty of a learning task depends to a great extent on the language development and personal experience of the student performing it. If a second language learner has to struggle to master lower-level language skills, she or he will be at a disadvantage when responding to tasks that require higher-order language skills. Furthermore, language difficulties are accentuated when a learning task provides little context that makes it clear and meaningful to the student.

Deeper understanding is needed of the English language skills required for academic learning in different subject areas and how those language skills differ from the skills used in informal communication in English. For example, Fillmore (1999) conducted an analysis of prototype test items in a high school graduation test used in one of the 26 states that require such examinations. The analysis showed that, to pass the test, students had to be able to do the following:

- Summarize and analyze texts to interpret meaning and assess the writer's use of language.
- Extract meaning from texts and relate it to other information.
- Evaluate evidence and arguments presented in texts and critique the logic of argument.
- Make grammatical corrections to text and combine sentences into more cohesive texts.
- Interpret word problems.
- Extract precise information to solve problems.
- Compose and write extended and reasoned text supported by details and evidence.

The English language demands given here would be challenging for many of today's high school students, but they are particularly demanding for English language learners. The level, depth, and intensity of language development that is necessary for students to acquire proficiency in academic English are not being sufficiently addressed in schools.

Language Development and the Implications for Teacher Preparation

Regular classroom teachers are pivotal in developing the English proficiency skills of language minority students and the academic skills necessary for success. The requirements of second language development add another dimension to the instructional decisions teachers have to make, and they call for strategies that specifically meet the needs of students who are developing second language proficiency. However, most teachers have not received adequate preparation and training to either organize or deliver instruction that is sensitive to the learning needs of English language learners. This situation is further complicated by the fact that regular classroom teachers often work in isolation from ESL/bilingual teachers who could provide expertise on strategies that support language development and learning for students not fully proficient in English. The complexity of teaching students at differing levels of language proficiency, combined with teacher isolation and the limited body of professional knowledge about effective teaching strategies, presents a major challenge to ensuring high quality instruction for English language learners who have been mainstreamed into regular classrooms (Ruiz de Velasco & Fix, 2000).

Fillmore & Snow (2000) suggested several areas of teacher preparation that are fundamental to the education of English language learners. These areas include:

Language and linguistics: Understanding language structure, the basics of linguistic analysis, language in literacy development, and language use in educational settings.

Language and cultural diversity: Cultural contrasts in language styles and how different discourse styles can be accommodated in a classroom.

Language development: Language development for native English speakers and those who speak other languages, and the role of literacy in developing language skills.

Second language learning: The role of the primary language in second language learning, factors that affect the acquisition of a second language, and levels of English language proficiency necessary to read and write.

The language of academic discourse: How language is used in subject-matter instruction in contrast to language use in informal communication.

Text analysis and language understanding: How language structures and style in written texts affect understanding and comprehensibility, and what aspects of text to target for instruction. (pp. 32–33)

The increasing diversity of the student population in America requires that all teachers develop deeper understandings about the role of culture and language in teaching and learning. Best-practice trends in the literature on reading instruction confirm the importance of linking new learnings to the prior knowledge and experiences of students, and integrating reading, writing, and critical thinking with content instruction wherever possible. This greater emphasis on more contextualized learning is important for all students, but it would also strengthen the process of how English language learners develop the language skills of reading, writing, listening, and speaking, and then apply those skills to content-area learning. Regular classroom teachers at all levels need much more preparation in this area. Long-term, school-based professional development is needed to increase teacher effectiveness with culturally and linguistically diverse students.

CHAPTER THREE

Applying Accountability Reforms

The 1994 reauthorization of the Elementary and Secondary Education Act (ESEA) was a response to the concerns of civil rights advocates that schools serving large numbers of poor, minority, and limited English proficient (LEP) students had set lower standards for the education of these groups and thus reinforced lower expectations for their performance. For the first time, a clear mandate had been established stating that high standards were to be the foundation of the education provided to English language learners (ELLs). The intent of the law was that standards-based learning and accountability would benefit these students by raising expectations for their achievement and improving the quality of instruction provided to them. While the 1994 mandates created the foundation for standards-based reform, the added requirements of the 2001 No Child Left Behind Act (NCLB) made schools accountable for the learning of all students in ways that are unprecedented.

The new act focuses on closing the achievement gap between minority students and their peers. The educational goal set for all schools is that 100% of the student population will demonstrate proficiency on standards-based state assessments by 2014. Part A of NCLB specifically describes the purposes of the act, including helping to ensure that "children who are limited English proficient, including immigrant children and youth, attain English proficiency; develop high levels of academic attainment in English; and meet the same challenging state academic content and student achievement standards as all children are expected to meet" (No Child Left Behind Act of 2001). The act also holds state education agencies, local education agencies, and schools accountable for increases in English proficiency and core academic knowledge. As English language learners become part of this legislated accountability system, their progress in developing essential proficiencies becomes a matter of public record.

THE PROMISE OF STANDARDS FOR ENGLISH LANGUAGE LEARNERS

The vision of school transformation that is driving the standards movement holds equal promise for all students—including poor students, ethnic minority students, and English language learners. The benefits are connected to higher expectations and the provision of higher quality instruction. Research and practice have demonstrated repeatedly that high expectations are essential to student success in school; that is, students do better when they know what is expected of them and when those expectations are high. It is equally recognized that when policymakers mandate high standards for student learning as the foundation for school accountability, schools pay attention. Federal and state policies that hold schools accountable for the progress of all students will be strong factors in motivating schools to raise performance expectations for previously underserved students, including English language learners. Putting standards at the core of their education should raise the bar of their achievement and overcome the long history of low expectations that have characterized their experiences in schools.

The NCLB legislation is sending a clear message that schools must create greater access to rich and varied educational opportunities for English language learners, or a large majority of these students will continue to perform at low levels. They must have access to the full range of knowledge and skills represented in higher learning standards and must be given instruction that adequately prepares them for assessments that require them to perform cognitively demanding learning tasks. This will require teachers to broaden the focus of instruction to include higher-order thinking and problem-solving processes in classroom activities for these students. Emerging strategies for assessing student learning through portfolios, exhibitions, projects, and careful observations of children's progress can strengthen teaching and learning by involving students in more meaningful and challenging work that integrates content from different subject areas; in addition, these strategies help teachers look more carefully at student work to understand how students are learning and thinking (Darling-Hammond, 1997). Because these strategies develop teachers' capacities to look closely at student work and reflect on students' strengths and needs, they offer promising approaches to improving the quality of teaching provided to English language learners.

Issues of Standards Implementation With English Language Learners

Numerous reports have indicated the need to include English language learners more centrally in reform efforts. Most of the studies on school reform have not addressed the issues faced by schools, teachers, and English language learners themselves in meeting the challenge of concurrently developing both English proficiency and academic proficiency in content areas. Standards-based reform has not adequately addressed the varied needs of English language learners, or the implications of emerging assessments for these students. "The implicit guiding assumption appears to be that whatever curricular revisions and/or assessment innovations contribute to the success of monolingual students will also work for ELLs—that once ELLs know a little English, the new and improved assessments will fit them too" (LaCelle-Peterson & Rivera, 1994, p. 56).

Researchers and advocates caution that the notion of "one size fits all" will not work, and that even the most promising approaches to instruction and assessment cannot be offered uniformly to all populations. Although having students perform the same task under the same conditions may seem like equity, school administrators and teachers must recognize that real equity requires diverse ways of solving problems and accomplishing tasks (Garcia & Pearson, 1994). Aligning the reform agenda in education with the research and practical wisdom on language development and instruction for English language learners must become a priority if these students are to succeed.

Concerns also exist about the use of standards with students who have not developed full English proficiency. Standards implementation rests on two important assumptions: that educators have the appropriate resources and know-how to implement the standards, and that most students are ready to perform at or near the desired performance level. These assumptions are not true for many schools and many classrooms, and they are particularly not true for schools and classrooms that serve English language learners. Two challenges are the wide diversity in the languages, literacy, and skills of these students; and the wide knowledge gaps in the education profession of how best to serve them (Ruiz de Velasco & Fix, 2000). Several studies, as well as data from state assessments, indicate that schools lack the capacity to make sure English language learners are performing at high levels.

Advocates for students with limited English proficiency have stressed that the standards-setting process has given too little consideration to *how* diverse student populations will meet the standards. The intent of the 1994 reauthorization of ESEA was that standards would guide reforms in curriculum and instruction and that by the 2000–2001 academic year all states would have assessments aligned with content and performance standards. The implementation of standards-based reforms in curriculum and instruction at the school and classroom levels has been painfully slow, however, and there are serious disconnects between the progress of school-level reform and the mandates of new state assessment systems. This factor alone has a serious impact on the education of all students (Menken, 2000). It has particular implications for the education provided to English language learners.

Many states have put standards implementation and assessments in place without providing the necessary level of support and teacher training. The standards do not provide guidance on how they should be implemented in the classroom with diverse learners; instead, teachers have to translate the concepts, skills, and processes embedded in content standards into instructional practices, but most are not prepared to do this. Effective standards implementation requires extensive professional development for teachers, as well as standards documents that are clear about how to connect the standards to best practices in teaching and learning.

In summary, applying standards equitably to diverse student populations requires that attention be paid to how standards can be linked to instructional practices at the classroom level, thus enabling students with varying levels of English proficiency to develop higher-level knowledge and skills. More attention must be given to the "nuts and bolts" of implementing standards at the classroom level and the accommodations that will be necessary for some children. Key issues are how all students can be included without dooming certain students to failure, and how differences can be accommodated without sacrificing academic rigor.

The TESOL ESL Standards—A Bridge
to Content-Area Standards

The ESL (English as a Second Language) standards, developed by Teachers of English to Speakers of Other Languages, Inc. (TESOL), were designed to be used in conjunction with content-specific standards for students who are still developing English proficiency. The ESL standards describe the language skills that are necessary for social and academic purposes, specifying the language competencies English language learners need in order to become fully proficient in English and to achieve success in challenging academic subjects. These standards articulate the English language development needs of English language learners, provide direction on how to meet the needs of these students, and highlight the central role of language in the attainment of content standards. They are intended to provide a bridge by helping teachers understand the unique instructional and assessment considerations that must be given to English language learners if these students are to benefit from and achieve the high standards of learning that are being proposed for various subject areas.

Spanning the preK–2 age levels, the ESL standards address three broad goals: (1) to use English to communicate in social settings; (2) to use English to achieve academically in all content areas; and (3) to use English in socially and culturally appropriate ways. For each standard, the following elements are provided:

Behavioral Descriptors: Representative behaviors that students exhibit when they meet a standard.

Progress Indicators: Assessable, observable activities for students to perform to show progress in meeting a standard.

Vignettes: Real classroom scenarios, drawn from the real-life experiences of teachers, that include instructional sequences or activities to demonstrate the standards in action and discussions that link the vignettes to the standards and progress indicators. (Teachers of English to Speakers of Other Languages, 1997)

The ESL standards were developed through a nationwide effort involving ESL teachers, language specialists, administrators, and researchers. They represent an important contribution to curriculum reform efforts aimed at promoting high levels of learning for English language learners. Most states and districts have also developed specific standards for English language learners as a complement to state content standards in the core subject areas of English language arts, mathematics, and science. Although there are considerable variations in the state ESL standards, most states and districts have modeled them primarily, or at least partially, on the TESOL standards (Menken & Holmes, 2000).

ASSESSMENT AND ACCOUNTABILITY FOR ENGLISH LANGUAGE LEARNERS

Historically, assessment policies that were not responsive to English language learners exerted a powerful influence over every aspect of their education. These policies determined how these students were identified and classified in the school population, their placement in the school program, and how their progress was monitored. How schools interpreted the performance of English language learners on various tests and assessments influenced both teacher beliefs about the abilities of these students and teacher expectations about the kinds of instruction these students should receive. As a result, assessment policies in most schools compounded the difficulties English language learners faced in their education and contributed to achievement gaps.

Garcia and Pearson (1994) highlighted the political aspect of discriminatory assessment policies:

At every level of analysis, assessment is a political act. Assessments tell people how they should value themselves and others. They open doors for some and close them for others. . . . The political dilemma is a problem for all students, but it is particularly acute for students from diverse cultural, linguistic, and economic backgrounds whose cultures, languages, and identities have been at best ignored and at worst betrayed in the assessment process. (p. 354)

Traditional testing policies and practices blocked educational opportunity for English language learners for four main reasons:

- Traditional testing was often culturally biased.
- Tests were not able to measure what English language learners knew.
- Test results led to inappropriate program placements.
- Minimal accountability data existed on the academic progress of English language learners because these students were often excluded from national and state assessment programs.

Because schools relied too heavily on test scores for program placement, English language learners were tracked into low-ability classrooms emphasizing rote learning and low cognitive tasks, with few opportunities to practice high-level thinking skills. This led to a self-perpetuating cycle where test scores placed ELL students into low-level educational settings where they received instruction that focused on low-level basic skills; subsequent test results were used to justify these placements. The type of education provided in these settings ensured that these students would not develop thinking and analytic skills.

In many cases, English language learners were also placed inappropriately in special education classes. Many school districts have, at times, confused the educational needs of students who are not proficient in English with the special education needs of students with disabilities (National Center on Accessing the General Curriculum, 2001). Based on results of tests that were administered in English and not designed with diverse cultural perspectives in mind, students who used languages other than English were misdiagnosed as having communication disorders. This misuse of assessments is still a concern, and a prevailing question is how to fairly assess children for possible disabilities when they are not proficient in the language of testing (Hernandez, 1994; National Center on Accessing the General Curriculum, 2001).

The gap is widening between the achievement scores of English language learners and those of mainstream English-speaking students. Students for whom English is a second language do not perform as well on national tests such as the National Assessment of Educational Progress (NAEP), and they are lagging behind their peers in their performance levels on standards-based state assessments. Discrepancies between the test scores of one group of students and those of another are caused in part by differences in the quality of education provided to them—differences that result from wide disparities in the financial resources available to schools, unequal access to high quality curriculum and instruction, educational practices that are aligned with the needs of one group of students but not those of another, and staff who are not prepared to teach students from different backgrounds (Darling-Hammond & Sykes, 1999; Williams, 1996). But test bias that favors mainstream student populations is also a part of the problem. Current measures for assessing the academic performance of LEP students at national and state levels are still not adequate to provide an accurate or reliable picture of their learning (Kopriva, 2000). In combination, these factors represent complex issues that will become far more pressing in the current context of accountability and standards-based assessment reform.

Inclusion in Assessments

LaCelle-Peterson and Rivera (1994) have highlighted the implications of two predominant approaches to assessing English language learners. In some cases, these students were tested without consideration of whether an assessment was technically valid for them as a student population. In other cases, they were excluded from assessments for a set period of time. LaCelle-Peterson and Rivera concluded that, by ignoring validity concerns, testing policies had failed to consider the educationally significant differences that distinguish English language learners from their monolingual peers. These authors also highlighted the fact that exempting English language learners from assessment programs creates widespread ignorance about their educational progress. Thus, while some educators and advocates for English language learners believe that they are overtested, in most cases these students have not been adequately assessed because what they know and can do has not been captured through national and state assessments.

Inclusion in National Assessments

Historically, national assessment programs have not provided adequate data on the academic progress of English language learners. Procedures used prior to 1990 for NAEP allowed schools to exclude a student who was part of the sample population if he or she was categorized as having limited English proficiency and if the local district judged this student incapable of participating meaningfully in the assessment. Beginning in 1990, NAEP defined in greater detail the conditions for excluding LEP students; more than two thirds of students identified as having limited proficiency in English were excluded from NAEP testing in 1992. Upon careful examination, it appeared that the exclusion criteria actually contributed to differences in exclusion rates across states participating in the NAEP Trial State Assessment because local district staff had different subjective interpretations (Olson & Goldstein, 1997).

Beginning with the 1995 NAEP field test, new procedures were put in place to include a more representative population of LEP students in the assessment sample. Inclusion criteria were revised to promote appropriate and consistent decisions about the inclusion of LEP students, and the field test employed various accommodations and adaptations in the mathematics assessment. Since 1995, a LEP student is included in NAEP if: (1) the student has received academic instruction primarily in English for at least three years; or (2) the student received academic instruction in English for fewer than three years, if school staff determine that the student is capable of participating in the assessment in English; or (3) the student, whose native language is Spanish, has received academic instruction in English for fewer than three years, if school staff determine the student is capable of participating in an assessment that is available in Spanish (Holmes & Duron, 2000). The 1995 NAEP also offered the following accommodations: extra testing time; modifications in the administration of sessions; facilitation in reading directions; and, for the mathematics sessions, the provision of Spanish-English bilingual assessment booklets and Spanish-only assessment booklets.

The findings from the 1995 NAEP field test indicated that, with the exception of the Spanish-only assessment booklets, the new procedures and accommodation strategies would permit the inclusion of more students in the national assessment, and they were incorporated in the 1996 NAEP assessment at the national level. It was also noted, however, that decisions about how to interpret and use the results of students tested with accommodations still needed to be addressed (Olson & Goldstein, 1997).

Inclusion in State Assessments

Prior to the standards movement, most states had not typically included students categorized as LEP in their assessment programs. Few states had developed clear inclusion policies, and there was a national need to improve policies for including these students in state assessments and in state accountability reports. The 1994 ESEA reauthorization addressed this need by mandating that standards and related assessments be applied to all students. By the end of the 2000–2001 school year, states were expected to have an assessment system in place that included English language learners in order to be sure they were making adequate yearly progress. Since 1994, there has been an increase in the participation of these students in state assessment programs. However, data compiled from state education agency reports and national surveys of state agencies indicated that high numbers of English language learners were still not included in any form of statewide assessments, resulting in no record of their progress in language development or their attainment of content-area skills (Menken, 2000). Typically, information about students who have been exempted from state assessments is not included in reports describing the results of the tested population. The problem with this approach is that test results are being used to evaluate the effectiveness of school programs; however, programs should be evaluated in terms of their effectiveness for all students, including those who have been exempted from the tests.

A major issue for states is the readiness of English language learners to take the state assessment because tests administered in English to these students can be more of an assessment of their English ability than their content knowledge. Because of this, states developed policies that exempted English language learners from statewide assessments based on three criteria: (1) their English proficiency level; (2) length of time in the United States; or (3) length of time enrolled in ESL/bilingual education programs (Goertz & Duffy, 2001; Holmes, Hedlund, & Nickerson, 2000).

A study conducted by Rivera (2000) showed that in 1998–99 almost all states had inclusion/exemption policies, but they generally provided minimal guidance to local districts and schools in how to use the criteria to make decisions about inclusion/exemption. Some states used a single criterion, whereas others used multiple criteria. Most states' policies also did not specify that a professional with expertise in language learning processes, such as an English as a Second Language teacher, should participate in the decisions. The conclusion of the study was that states needed to revise existing policies to be better aligned with current legislation and best practices.

There is no simple solution to the inclusion of English language learners in state assessments. Issues related to fairness in assessment and the need to include them in the process of assessment development have not been given sufficient attention. Although inclusion is clearly beneficial from an accountability perspective, it is not clear whether their immediate inclusion in high-stakes assessments is beneficial if the assessments are not appropriate, valid, or reliable (August & McArthur, 1996). On the other hand, when English language learners are exempted from assessments, no one is held accountable for their progress, and the assessed population is not representative of the total student population because a significant segment has not been included (August & Hakuta, 1997; Holmes & Duron, 2000; Lara & August, 1996; Rivera & Stansfield, 1998; Rivera & Vincent, 1997). Issues are further complicated by the fact that many states are already using the results of new state assessment programs to make decisions about placement, grade promotion, and high school graduation. English language learners are particularly vulnerable to these high-stakes decisions (Heubert & Hauser, 1999).

ASSESSMENT REFORM AND ENGLISH LANGUAGE LEARNERS

Although new state assessment systems are the primary vehicle for ensuring and demonstrating accountability, there are genuine concerns that English language learners have been kept on the periphery of assessment reform. State assessment programs have been developed without sufficiently addressing, first, the linguistic and cultural factors that have an impact on validity and fairness in assessment, and, second, how test results for students who are not fully proficient in English will be used for accountability purposes. The central question is whether state assessments measure content for English language learners as effectively as they measure the same content for mainstream students.

> Assessment policy is not about whether to include, exclude, or exempt English language learners from assessments. Rather, the discussion must center around two questions: how best to assess English language learners, and how best to incorporate the data into accountability assessments of schools and school systems. (LaCelle-Peterson & Rivera, 1994, p. 68)

Fairness and Equity in State Assessments

Achieving fairness and equity for English language learners in state assessment programs presents multiple challenges that are tied to these students' widely varying characteristics, the influence of language and culture on their learning, and the quality of education provided to them. In the assessment debate surrounding the participation of English language learners in high-stakes state assessments, researchers and educators have identified several core issues:

- Are non-mainstream students who represent a wide continuum of cultural and linguistic diversity being given adequate preparation in the proficiencies assessed in state assessment programs?
- At what point can preliterate English language learners with limited and/or interrupted schooling be expected to reach established standards?
- Are the designs of new assessments responsive to cultural and linguistic diversity and the complexity of

assessing students with widely varying levels of language proficiency?

- At what point along the language proficiency continuum does performance on a high-stakes assessment yield valid results, and to what extent are test results for English language learners valid when language proficiency is being assessed in addition to content matter?
- How can students with varying levels of English language proficiency be effectively accommodated in states' assessments, and to what extent are the results of tests taken with accommodations comparable to the mainstream tests results?
- How can rubrics and scoring procedures be developed that accurately measure student performance and distinguish between errors due to language proficiency and those related to content or skill knowledge?
- What are the best methods of reporting and interpreting scores? (Holmes & Duron, 2000)

These issues go beyond the fundamental issue of ensuring inclusion. They point to measurement issues in assessing students from non-mainstream cultures in ways that show what these students actually know and can do, and equity issues in how the data will be used by schools. A major need exists to address these issues and to increase the validity of tests for English language learners while still being able to collect comparable and generalizable information across population subgroups (Kopriva, 2000).

Representation in Assessment Development

Farr and Trumbull (1997) caution that new assessment practices may have limited utility for English language learners because of the common practice of getting reforms in place for "the majority" and then trying to adapt them to "special populations," often after financial and human resources have been exhausted. They argue that assessment development should focus on special populations first. Instead, states have developed and field tested new assessments for the general population, allowing the technical demands of test construction to postpone consideration of whether these new assessments are appropriate and fair for English language learners. Once developed, tests are then reviewed to determine whether a native-language version or some type of accommodation would facilitate the participation of English language learners.

Addressing the needs of English language learners as an afterthought makes it more difficult to develop assessments that are inclusive, valid, and reliable for this population. Making inferences about the competencies of English language learners from assessments that have been validated with monolingual English-speaking students constitutes an invalid use of assessment data. They need to be included in the field-test population. A "best practice" approach in the development of assessment instruments and procedures is to field test them with a student sample that is representative of all the types of students who will take the assessment (Olson & Goldstein, 1997).

Instead of adjusting assessments to English language learners after their development, educators and assessment specialists with substantive knowledge of these students should be active participants during the development of the assessment policies, test construct and framework, items and tasks, rubrics and scoring, and test procedures (National Clearinghouse for Bilingual Education, 1997; Olson & Goldstein, 1997). The input of such individuals is also essential to decisions about test reporting and the use of test results. Kopriva (2000) urges the expanded use of bias reviews by test developers that provide opportunities for representatives of special populations such as English language learners to review and comment on test materials in such areas as test formats, wording in items and directions, scoring parameters, and the accessibility of test items in terms of what students need to understand in order to respond to the item.

Cultural Bias Issues

A major issue in the current context of high-stakes accountability is the validity of standards-based assessments in measuring the academic achievement of English language learners. The central concern is whether new state assessment systems will provide an adequate picture of what English language learners actually know and can do. While testing programs have been limited in the extent to which they adequately measure any student's higher cognitive abilities, they have been particularly limiting for English language learners because tests written in English cannot adequately assess the content knowledge of these students. A key issue relates to *content* or *cultural bias.* Content bias occurs when a test's content and procedures reflect the language structure and shared knowledge of the mainstream culture or when test items do not include activities, words, or concepts familiar to non-mainstream students. "It is most severe when test tasks, topics, and vocabulary reflect the culture of mainstream society to such an extent that it is difficult to do well on a formal test without being culturally assimilated" (Garcia & Pearson, 1994, p. 344). Content bias controls a student's understanding of the proficiency that is being assessed, and it is as much an issue in the development of standards-based assessments as it was in the development of traditional standardized measures.

Because assessment reform does not automatically eradicate test bias, the lack of focus on English language learners in assessment reform has heightened concerns that the greater reliance on language-dependent skills and situational contexts in performance-based assessments may actually increase the sources of cultural bias in emerging assessment programs. Moreover, critical-thinking tasks that involve making judgments or expressing values may go against the norms of some cultural groups. Garcia and Pearson (1994) point out that experts in multicultural education have shown how difficult it is for mainstream educators to identify topics that are culturally relevant to minority students, and that even the involvement of minority educators in selecting and developing topics, tasks, and rubrics cannot guarantee an assessment's fairness to a particular minority population. Developing performance tasks that can fairly assess students who approach problems from distinct cultural perspectives is a complex challenge with significant implications for whether state and national assessments will be valid and fair for English language learners (Holmes & Duron, 2000).

The technical demands of test construction, from developing test items to establishing reliability in scoring, are typically given precedence over the need to ensure that tests are both valid and fair for all tested student populations (Wolf et al., 1991). Admittedly, a few items on any test are likely to be unfair to some students. When students' cultural, language, and economic backgrounds and frames of reference are not considered by the test developers, however, the result is that these students face a disproportionate number of test items that are unfair to them, and test results must be considered invalid for these students.

Performance-based assessments, which call for students to use background knowledge and reasoning strategies to make judgments and to analyze and solve problems, only make validity an even more complex issue. Many English language learners draw on life experiences that differ from those who develop assessments and thus may respond to performance assessments in unanticipated ways. Therefore, although new assessments offer many potential advantages, "many forms of bias will remain, as the choice of items, responses deemed appropriate, and content deemed important are the product of culturally and contextually determined judgments, as well as the privileging of certain ways of knowing and modes of performance over others" (Darling-Hammond, 1994, p. 17). To ensure that current reform efforts create assessments that are fair and valid for English language learners, linguistic and cultural factors must be weighed *during* the assessment development process. The diverse cultural backgrounds represented in a student population and the amount of knowledge of mainstream culture needed to understand and respond to an assessment item or task should be considered when developing assessments (Winfield, 1995).

Language Issues

Another critical issue in the assessment of English language learners is determining the point at which students have developed sufficient proficiency in English to ensure that the results they achieve on a high-stakes test represents an accurate picture of their achievement (National Clearinghouse for Bilingual Education, 1997). Two major language issues relate to: (1) the difficulties posed by unfamiliar vocabulary; and (2) the difficulty of assessing student literacy on a variety of language skills.

> *Difficulties posed by unfamiliar english vocabulary:* Unfamiliar English vocabulary poses difficulties for English language learners, and they are at a disadvantage when knowledge of uncommon terms is essential for understanding test instructions, an item, or a passage. Whenever students who are still in the process of learning English take tests written in English, regardless of the content or intent of the test, their proficiency in English will also be tested. As a result, such tests may be invalid or unreliable measures of English language learners' academic proficiencies (American Education Research Association, American Psychological Association, & National Council of Measurement in Education, 1999).

> *Difficulty of assessing a variety of language skills:* The development of essential literacy skills is a major focus of the NCLB legislation as well as of state education reform efforts. However, the proficiency of English language learners in the distinct language skills of reading, writing, speaking, and listening can be difficult to determine. A student's skills may vary considerably across these separate areas of language competence. Furthermore, proficiency in one's

native language may influence a student's ability to develop competency across these areas, as well as the ability to learn new content in either language (Clements, Lara, & Cheung, 1992). While research indicates that a student's first language is an important resource that contributes to second language development and improvement of thinking skills, current measures do not assess learning that draws upon the interactions of two languages (August & Hakuta, 1997).

In determining when an assessment will yield meaningful results for English language learners, some researchers have suggested the need for language development profiles showing a student's status along a second-language-acquisition continuum. Movement along the continuum would start with students who are preliterate in both English and their native language, would move to students who are literate in their native language but who have very limited exposure to or proficiency in English, and would end with students who are sufficiently fluent in English that testing would yield valid results (Collier, 1995; McLaughlin & McLeod, 1996).

Issues in the Use of Performance Tasks on State Assessments

The incorporation of performance tasks in state assessments introduces some new equity issues that can influence the scoring of student proficiency. Potential inequities relate to: (1) the nature of performance assessment tasks that are richer but cover fewer topics; (2) biases in how performance assessments are scored; and (3) differences in how assessments are administered.

Fewer tasks and longer reading passages: When large-scale assessment programs incorporate more complex performance tasks, fewer topics can be surveyed by the test. Questions have been raised about how the limited number of topics will affect the scores of culturally diverse student populations. Emerging performance assessments generally present students with a few longer passages rather than a wide range of short reading passages. By using longer passages, performance assessments seek to provide students with more meaningful and authentic opportunities to demonstrate what they know and can do. However, reading longer passages may be particularly difficult for English language learners, and judgments about the proficiency levels of these students that are based on a more limited sampling of tasks or passages may lead to incorrect inferences about their actual capabilities (Garcia & Pearson, 1994).

An assessment that draws on a limited number of assessment tasks increases the likelihood that some children may have had little exposure to the limited content reflected in the assessments (Estrin & Nelson-Barber, 1995). It is, therefore, possible that a limited range of topics will not provide adequate opportunities for diverse student populations to demonstrate what their knowledge and abilities. It increases the likelihood that student scores may be more of an indicator of mainstream cultural experience than actual competencies in the content matter being assessed.

Scoring rubrics and bias: Whether the results of performance assessments of English language learners are reliable or not will depend on how scoring rubrics are developed and how much bias affects the scoring of assessments. The scorers of student responses to performance assessments are expected to apply clearly defined performance criteria to make a sound judgment about the level of proficiency demonstrated. Even in large-scale performance assessments, however, only a small number of teachers participate in the design of scoring rubrics. Therefore, the reliability of performance criteria can be undermined if those who design scoring rubrics are not knowledgeable about how to teach and assess children from a variety of cultural and linguistic backgrounds. (Baker & O'Neil, 1995)

Although research has shown that well-trained raters working with well-defined and articulated scoring criteria can reach high levels of agreement with one another, ratings of student performance can be subject to scorer biases based on observable attributes such as a student's ethnicity and gender. "Even when relatively structured rubrics are used, there is some evidence that raters rate members of their own race or ethnicity higher than those of other races and ethnicities" (Baker & O'Neil, 1995, p. 73). In addition, when student performance on a demonstration or exhibition is assessed, it can be heavily influenced by scorer response to students' verbal skills, dialect, or accent. "In many cases, individuals who speak in dialects or with accents are more likely to be judged as less intelligent and less capable" (Garcia & Pearson, 1994, p. 228).

> *Assessment administration:* How performance assessments are administered is likely to vary from one school or classroom to the next. Differences in procedures such as directions to tasks, the types of help provided, and the availability of resources can have a significant impact on the performance of English language learners in a testing situation and on the results they achieve. Therefore, the context in which a performance-based assessment is administered will affect the validity of the results for English language learners (Baker & Linn, 2002).

Use of Accommodations

States permit supportive accommodations to increase the participation of English language learners in content assessments, and they provide these students with the opportunity to sufficiently demonstrate skills and knowledge. Some of the accommodations are designed to reduce the English language demand (by creating options that reduce the difficulty of reading/understanding students may experience), while others permit alternative settings for taking the test and allow more flexible time options. A study of state policies conducted by Rivera and Stansfield (2000) classified accommodations into four main types:

Presentation: Permits repetition, explanation, test translations into students' native languages, or test administration by an ESL/bilingual specialist.

Response: Allows a student to dictate his or her answers and to respond in his or her native language.

Setting: Includes individual or small-group administration of the test, or administration in a separate location.

Timing/scheduling: Allows for additional time to complete the test or extra breaks during administration.

The Rivera and Stansfield study, as well as an analysis of state reports on accommodations (Holmes et al., 2000), showed that the most commonly used accommodations fell into the categories of setting and timing/scheduling, which do not address the linguistic needs of English language learners. Presentation and response options, which do provide some type of language support, are less commonly permitted. Rivera and Vincent (1996) have cautioned that accommodations do not work equally well for all English language learners because of wide variations in English language proficiency. While accommodations may make a positive difference for English language learners who already are fairly proficient in English, for those who have very little proficiency in English the accommodations may not make enough of a difference to enable students to perform at high performance levels.

An issue for states is whether the results of tests taken with accommodations can be compared to the results of tests taken without accommodations. This issue of consistency or comparability across tests will not be resolved easily from a technical standpoint. Researchers and technical experts have suggested that the assessment results of students who take an assessment without accommodations should be separated from those students who take the assessment with accommodations. The use of alternative assessment strategies and accommodations requires research, analysis, and evaluation of assessment practices to determine their comparability to the assessments used to measure the progress of fluent English speakers. States can learn from empirical studies, conducted by the National Center for Research on Evaluation, Standards, and Student Testing (CRESST), that examine the inclusion of LEP students in the NAEP, as well as research efforts by CRESST researchers that focus specifically on the validity of accommodations and modifications in assessments. The findings of these CRESST studies should have important implications for the large-scale use of assessment accommodations and modifications.

Use of Translated Versions of Assessments

Because of the high proportion of English language learners who come from Spanish-language backgrounds, some states with a large and stable population of these students are developing Spanish versions of content-area assessments that can be offered as an assessment option. While the limitations of English-only assessments are becoming increasingly obvious, however, translating a test from one language to another raises many new issues. Because concepts and terminology do not have perfect equivalents in different languages, translated items may exhibit psychometric properties substantially different from those of the original English items. Thus, a translated test may not effectively test the same underlying concepts and competencies (Cabello, 1984; Farr & Trumball, 1997). Also, because some languages, such as Spanish, have many dialects, it can be very difficult to translate material in a way that will be similarly understood by most speakers of the language (Estrin, 1993). The 1985 Standards for Educational and Psychological Testing noted the difficulties presented by translation. Psychometric properties cannot be assumed to be comparable across languages or dialects. Many words have different frequency rates or difficulty levels in different languages or dialects. Therefore, words in two languages that appear to be close in meaning may differ radically in other ways in terms of how they are used in a test item. Additionally, test content may be inappropriate in a translated version.

Furthermore, problems occur in developing effective native-language assessments because many English language learners have developed only limited literacy and language skills in their primary languages and therefore need to use both the native language version and English language version of the test. Developing and validating equivalent "bilingual" versions of a test (two versions side by side) is very difficult. For example, research results from the 1995 NAEP field test of mathematics, which tested items in Spanish-only or in side-by-side Spanish-English formats, illustrated the challenge of using native language or bilingual versions of assessments (Anderson, Jenkins, & Miller, 1996). Researchers found substantial psychometric discrepancies in students' performance on the same test items across both languages, leading to the conclusion that the Spanish and English versions of many test items were not measuring the same underlying mathematical knowledge (August & Hakuta, 1997).

Because direct translation may actually introduce more language bias, the most highly recommended procedure in test translation is *back translation*. In this procedure, the test that has been translated into the second language is translated back into English. The two English versions are compared, and items showing apparent discrepancies in vocabulary, phrasing, or meaning are modified further in the translated version. When this process is completed, the newly revised version goes through another back translation. At least three back translations, each conducted by a different translator, are generally recommended in order to prepare a translated assessment that does not introduce inadvertent discrepancies in meaning (Lam, 1991).

ACHIEVING EQUITY IN ASSESSMENT FOR ENGLISH LANGUAGE LEARNERS

Because adequate resources have never been devoted to addressing issues of assessment for English language learners, many more questions than answers about policies and practices should be followed when including English language learners in large-scale statewide assessment programs. While the knowledge base is limited, however, many studies are underway, and three overall principles have been highlighted (August & McArthur, 1996).

Maximum Inclusion: Assessment results should represent all students. Every student, regardless of language characteristics, should be included in the assessment population.

A Continuum of Strategies: Because no single strategy will enable all English language learners to participate fairly in large-scale assessment programs, a continuum of options should be available to support the participation of these students. These options may include those that have been proven to be effective, as well as untested options that still need to be field tested. Researchers suggest that assessment programs should draw on available options and attempt to maximize the number of students who are offered options on the tested/proven end of the continuum. At the same time, the feasibility and impact of untested options should be investigated. The rationale is that the use of the entire range of options would allow the inclusion of more students and would provide the opportunity to examine strategies that foster meaningful assessment and broader accountability.

Practicality: Assessments designed to meet the needs of English language learners must be evaluated for their costs, benefits, consequences, and feasibility of their administration. For example, since it is not always feasible to develop native language assessments because of the costs and psychometric problems involved in getting an equivalent translation of a test from one language to another, other ways of assessing English language learners who are not proficient in English need to be explored. Alternative assessment strategies must also take into account whether the requirements and burdens of assessment administration are manageable at the local level and whether the toll of assessment on individual test takers is too great.

Many factors must be considered in achieving inclusive and equitable assessment for English language learners. These include the prior knowledge and language skills that assessment tasks require; whether test content, procedures, or scoring criteria are biased; whether tests are valid for the population being assessed; and whether all students have had the opportunity to learn the material assessed. Each of these factors presents a score of issues yet to be resolved. In addition, these factors are interrelated and influence one another. The following section contains a set of questions that can be used as guidelines in examining the equity, fairness, and validity of assessments.

GUIDING QUESTIONS FOR ACHIEVING EQUITY AND FAIRNESS IN ASSESSMENT FOR ENGLISH LANGUAGE LEARNERS

Opportunity to Learn

- Have all students had the opportunity to learn the assessed material and to prepare adequately to respond to the assessment tasks?

- Have English language learners been placed in challenging learning situations that are organized around a full range of educational outcomes?
- Have all students been taught by teachers of the same quality, training, and experience?
- What educational resources are available to students? Are comparable books, materials, technology, and other educational supports available to all groups to be tested?

Validity

- Is the test valid for the school populations being assessed? Has the assessment been validated with culturally and linguistically diverse student populations?
- Does the assessment take into account the cultural backgrounds of the students taking the test?
- Have all test translations been validated and normed?

Relevant Prior Knowledge

- What common experiences and understandings must students have in order to make sense of the assessment task and solve it?
- Can students connect their cultural background and experiences to what is expected in the task?
- Will all groups be motivated by the topics provided?
- What information is essential for successful performance?
- Are the criteria for performance known and familiar to all students; that is, do all students understand what kind of evidence of learning will be valued when the assessment is scored?

Language Demands and Content Bias

- What language demands do the tasks—particularly those emphasizing higher-order thinking skills—place on students with backgrounds in languages other than English?

- If the task is not primarily meant to assess language facility, what alternative options for displaying understanding are available to students with limited English proficiency?
- Are the concepts, vocabulary, and activities important to the assessment tasks familiar to all students to be tested, regardless of their cultural backgrounds?
- Are the range of knowledge and ways of expressing knowledge called for in the assessment familiar only to the mainstream culture?
- Are the limited topics used in performance assessments relevant to students with many different backgrounds?

Procedural Bias and Scoring Criteria

- Do assessments unduly penalize students for whom the testing format is unfamiliar or for whom the prescribed time limitations are inadequate because of unfamiliarity with the test language?
- Are English language learners given sufficient time to complete an assessment?
- Do language differences, cultural attitudes toward test taking, lack of experience with tests, or test anxiety unduly penalize some students?
- What accommodations would be necessary to give English language learners the same opportunity that monolingual students have to demonstrate what they know and can do?
- Are the scoring criteria used to judge student performance biased toward the mainstream culture?
- Do scoring criteria for content-area assessments focus on the knowledge, skills, and abilities being tested and not on the quality of the language in which the response is expressed?
- Are the criteria specific enough to overcome the potential for bias when multiple raters are used to judge the performance of a group of students?

- Are those scoring the assessment sufficiently familiar with students' cultural and linguistic backgrounds to interpret student performances appropriately and to recognize and score English language learners' responses?
- Does the array of raters scoring students' work include educators from the same linguistic and cultural backgrounds as the students tested? (August & Hakuta, 1997; Baker & Linn, 2002; Baker & O'Neil, 1995; FairTest, 2000; Fair & Trumbull, 1997; Holmes & Duron, 2000; Kopriva, 2000; Olson & Goldstein, 1997; Rivera & Vincent, 1997)

Equity in the Use of Assessment Results

At the center of the education reform debate lie questions about the choices policymakers and school leaders make about the use of assessment results. Will the test results be used to determine student placements, reinforce differentiated curriculum tracking, and allocate rewards and sanctions to schools? Or will they primarily be used to enhance teaching and learning and to increase educational opportunity for students who have traditionally been served poorly by public education? Today, because of financial and political demands, legislators and educators are demanding that the same assessment system serve incompatible purposes. These conflicting purposes have produced a tension at the heart of assessment reform.

A perennial problem of testing programs is that policymakers and others wish to use a single instrument for a multitude of purposes—for example, to foster good teaching and learning, to make high-stakes decisions about individuals, to hold schools and districts accountable, to facilitate a voucher system, and to monitor national progress toward realizing federal, state, and local educational goals. Long experience with issues of test design, scoring, reporting, and the need for a supporting infrastructure teaches that these different purposes require different procedures and techniques. (Madaus, 1994, p. 88)

Policymakers and educational leaders must understand the implications of their choices, for new forms of assessment "will not be powerful or useful tools unless those who use them have a fundamental understanding of and belief in the views of learning and knowing to which they are conceptually linked" (Farr & Trumbull, 1997, p. 26). When policy decisions are made without clearly evaluating the intended purpose and use of assessment, unintended consequences result that are destructive to children. These consequences can be particularly harmful to the children who represent social, cultural, and linguistic diversity.

CHAPTER FOUR

Implementing Standards-Based Learning With English Language Learners

Standards-based learning presents significant opportunities for students and significant challenges for schools. The vision and mandates of "high standards for all" require schools to provide all students with access to the full range of content knowledge that is valued by society. Standards-based learning means that the curriculum for all students is based on the same expectations of what students should know and be able to do. Assessment is integrated with instruction, subject matter is organized around real-world tasks, and the pace of instruction is based on student progress rather than how much content has to be "covered." Schools are expected to provide the level of instruction that enables all students to acquire essential proficiencies. Emphasis is on results, decreased use of textbook "end-of-unit" tests and norm-referenced measures, and increased use of alternative assessments that offer ways for students to demonstrate their understanding and skills. This shift toward standards-based learning represents a very different mission for schools by demanding higher quality educational programs and accountability for the success of all students. Changes for schools that are embedded in standards-based learning are shown in Figure 4.1.

Figure 4.1   Comparison of traditional and new paradigms for schools

Traditional School Paradigm	New Paradigm for School
• The "inputs" and process of education are emphasized over results. Curriculum is "covered," and instruction is organized around limited time units prescribed by the school schedule. Schools accept the failure of a significant number of students.	• The school mission emphasizes high levels of learning for all students. Diverse abilities, developmental levels, readiness, and learning styles are addressed so that all can succeed. There is flexibility in the use of instructional time, with an emphasis on learning rather than how much content has to be "covered."
• The curriculum is derived from existing content, often determined by textbooks. The curriculum is organized around a set of units, sequences, concepts, and facts.	• The curriculum is derived from standards that define essential knowledge in content areas. Subject matter is "integrated" around "real-world" tasks that require reasoning, problem solving, and communication.
• Learning is organized around a standardized curriculum delivered in standardized time periods. Credentials are awarded based on "time served," issued in "Carnegie Units."	• Learning is organized around what students should know and be able to do. Credentialing is based on student demonstration of proficiency in these knowledge and skill areas.

• Assessment is done at the end of instruction and is narrowly focused on lower-level and fragmented (end-of-unit) skills that can be assessed through paper-pencil responses. There is minimal systematic monitoring of student progress on an ongoing basis.	• Assessment is integrated with instruction and focuses on what students understand and can do. Methods assess students' competencies through demonstrations, portfolios of work, and other measures. Emphasis is on frequent monitoring of student progress.
• School accountability is defined in terms of programs offered, attendance and dropout rates, and the number of students who are credentialed. Norm-referenced standardized test results are the basis of accountability.	• The school is accountable for showing that all students are developing proficiencies that represent high-level standards for what students should know and be able to do. State-based assessments are the basis of accountability.
• School improvement focuses are on improving the existing organization, adding new programs, changing textbooks, offering teacher workshops, improving school climate, and increasing staff participation in decision making.	• The emphasis is on systemic reform of school structures, the curriculum, and instructional practices. Collaborative leadership and continuous professional development are emphasized. Improvement is based on sound data about student learning and achievement.

Source: Lachat, 1994; Lachat & Williams, 1999.

ADVANTAGES OF STANDARDS-BASED LEARNING FOR ENGLISH LANGUAGE LEARNERS

It is important for teachers to recognize that the core elements of standards-based learning approaches are highly advantageous to English language learners (ELLs). These core elements include:

- Challenging and engaging instruction
- Authentic learning tasks
- Connecting content material to students' lives and experiences
- Emphasis on a student-centered learning environment
- Deeper examination of student work
- Increased focus on literacy and the language demands of content-based learning

Challenging and Engaging Instruction

When high standards drive classroom instruction for English language learners, it is far more likely that learning activities will be stimulating and thought provoking, with more flexibility to develop essential knowledge and skills over extended periods of time. The focus on real-world tasks creates opportunities to make connections to the life experiences of English language learners. In standards-based learning environments, holistic concepts rather than fragmented units of information are emphasized. A wider range of resources are used, and students participate in collaborative learning activities. Standards-based learning requires new skills of students and teachers and new roles in the learning process. The overall emphasis on higher-order reasoning and problem-solving skills means that the learning process encourages attention to how students think and what they understand.

What teachers do in standards-based learning:

- Organize learning around what students need to know and be able to do.

- Broaden the focus of their teaching to include higher-order thinking processes.
- Guide student inquiry by posing tasks that require real-life reasoning and problem solving.
- Emphasize holistic concepts rather than fragmented units of information.
- Provide a variety of opportunities for students to explore and confront concepts and situations over time.
- Use multiple sources of information rather than a single text.
- Work in interdisciplinary teams.
- Use multiple forms of assessment to gather concrete evidence of student proficiencies.

What students do in standards-based learning:

- Develop reasoning and problem-solving skills through real-world learning tasks.
- Play an active role in "constructing" their own understanding of concepts.
- Explore issues and concepts in depth over time.
- Make connections to their life experiences.
- Take increased responsibility for their learning.
- Use a wide range of resources including manipulatives and computer technology.
- Participate in collaborative-learning activities that allow them to learn from interactions with peers and teachers.
- Continually demonstrate their understanding and proficiency in knowledge and skill areas. (Lachat, 1999a)

Standards-based learning approaches hold great promise for improving the academic achievement of English language learners. English language learners will learn more effectively when instructional tasks are both meaningful and challenging, and if they are active participants in structuring their own learning. Figure 4.2 depicts a range of potential benefits for English language learners, identified by Laturnau (2001), based on a paradigm of standards-based learning.

Figure 4.2   Benefits of standards-based learning for English
language learners

In standards-based instruction, teachers . . .	The potential benefits for ELLs are that this paradigm shift . . .
Organize learning around what students need to know and be able to do to reach high levels of performance.	Has the potential to reverse the tendency to assign ELLs to unchallenging curricula, and presents an opportunity for schools to engage in substantive communication with the parents of ELLs regarding achievement.
Broaden the focus of their teaching to include higher-order thinking processes.	Sets high learning expectations for ELLs, who have traditionally been provided with instruction focusing on low-level skills.
Guide student inquiry by giving students work related to real-life tasks that require reasoning and problem solving.	Allows ELLs to build upon their prior knowledge and provides for diverse ways of solving problems.
Emphasize holistic concepts rather than fragmented units of information.	Focuses more on how ELLs think and what they understand rather than on whether or not they have the one right answer.
Provide a variety of opportunities for students to explore and develop their understanding of concepts and situations over time.	Helps teachers understand how ELLs learn; places value on the linguistic and cultural backgrounds of ELLs; and allows ELLs to draft, reflect on, and revise their work.
Use multiple sources of information rather than a single text.	Allows for a variety of learning styles and offers multiple pathways and connections to academic success.
Work in interdisciplinary teams.	Improves communication between regular education and ELL staff, and encourages an open dialogue about a school's expectations for ELLs.
Use multiple forms of assessment to gather concrete evidence of student proficiencies and achievement.	Complements diverse ways of knowing and learning and reveals productive "entry points" that build on students' strengths and lead to new areas of learning.

Sources: Lachat, 1999a; Laturnau, 2001.

Authentic Learning Tasks

English language learners have a far better chance of succeeding in school if learning tasks connect to their cultural frames of reference and their personal experiences. Therefore, the standards movement's emphasis on authentic learning tasks can benefit these students by allowing them to apply essential knowledge to contexts that are meaningful. This emphasis on context is even more important for the English language learner who has to demonstrate content knowledge in an emerging second language. Authentic learning tasks that invite English language learners to solve real problems provide them with more control over their learning.

The more that instructional processes draw upon the real-life experiences of English language learners, allow them to build on their prior knowledge, and allow for diverse ways of solving problems, the easier it will be for them to demonstrate what they know and can do. This doesn't mean that learning should be limited to the experiences that students bring to school, but rather that these experiences serve as starting points for making knowledge meaningful. The student's home culture can be an asset in the learning process, and, when designing learning tasks for English language learners, teachers can integrate home and community experiences into instruction. The challenge is making effective instructional use of the personal and cultural knowledge of students, while at the same time helping them reach beyond their cultural boundaries (Banks & Banks, 1993).

Issues for Teachers in Developing Culturally Relevant Tasks

In developing learning tasks for English language learners, teachers face two challenges—developing a task that is "authentic" to students from different cultures, as well as developing a task that requires students to demonstrate higher-order learning skills. Using performance tasks fairly in a classroom with students from diverse cultural and language backgrounds means that teachers have to become knowledgeable both about the subject matter being assessed and about students' cultures and languages.

It is not easy for mainstream educators to identify culturally relevant topics. Therefore, the greater reliance on situational contexts in higher-order learning tasks could actually increase cultural bias. The issue is whether the "real-world" situations of learning tasks are the "real world" of students from different cultures.

When a teacher is responsible for students from different cultures, there is always the question of whether the topics of learning tasks are culturally relevant, and whether learning activities enable students to bridge the differences between their own backgrounds and the academic knowledge valued in schools. Attention must also be given to determining the requisite mainstream cultural knowledge necessary for understanding and responding to a learning task. When teachers do not consider how students' cultural backgrounds affect their ways of working on a task, these teachers tend to form expectations about how a task should be completed that lead to false impressions about student abilities. This is complicated by the fact that teachers have typically not been trained in developing or assessing performance-based authentic learning tasks, even for mainstream students. Because of this, teachers form impressions of students too quickly and inaccurately. Schools need to recognize the probability of cultural bias (versus cultural relevance) of learning tasks at the classroom level, and they need to provide teachers with the professional development that will enable them to recognize cultural relevance.

Resources produced by the Northeast and Islands Regional Educational Laboratory at Brown University (LAB) describe the following seven principles of culturally responsive teaching for English language learners and the strategies that support effective implementation: (1) having positive perspectives on parents and families of culturally and linguistically diverse students; (2) communicating high expectations;

(3) connecting culture to school learning; (4) encouraging student-centered learning that actively engages students; (5) having culturally mediated instruction that incorporates diverse ways of knowing, understanding, and representing information; (6) reshaping the curriculum to reflect students' backgrounds and experiences; and (7) using the teacher as a facilitator to guide student learning (Northeast and Islands LAB, 2002).

Emphasis on a Student-Centered Learning Environment

The advantage for all students in a standards-based learning environment is that the learner is at the center of the process, the orientation to instruction is based on high expectations for all students, and instructional strategies are flexible and designed to actively engage students. Nevertheless, creating a classroom that is responsive to linguistically diverse students requires a culturally sensitive teacher who can help students bridge the ways of thinking and knowing that are shaped by their home culture and the expectations of standards-based learning. When teachers combine standards-based instructional practices with a proactive effort to draw on students' home cultures in the learning process, classrooms can become dynamic and effective learning environments for English language learners. Students learn better when they are encouraged to discuss the concepts they are learning and relate them to their own experiences, share their thoughts and ideas with other students, and ask questions. In a student-centered classroom, progress is positively reinforced, and students are given opportunities to demonstrate or exhibit their work.

Deeper Examination of Student Work

Standards-based learning requires a focus on desired results as well as the development of benchmarks and sample student products that convey to students what success looks like. Because these evaluative criteria are shared from the beginning and are often created with student input, it becomes easier for English language learners to internalize expectations for learning. Student work samples can provide concrete examples of what students know and do not know. Multiple forms of assessment can be used to gather evidence of student proficiencies, and students can be provided with a variety of ways to demonstrate what they have learned, such as performing on-demand tasks, presenting exhibitions of their work, preparing long-term projects, or assembling portfolios that contain a collection of their work produced over time.

These strategies develop teachers' capacities to look closely at student work and reflect on students' strengths and needs. They require teachers to look more carefully at how students are learning and thinking, and they focus teachers' attention on the actual results of their teaching in contrast to what they assume students have learned. There is also great power in having teachers examine student work as a team, as teachers can learn from each other's perspectives on "quality work" and determine if there are discrepancies in teachers' criteria for success. The ongoing examination of student work also helps in keeping an awareness of the cultural relevance of a learning task in the forefront, and it fosters an awareness of equity issues in scoring the work of English language learners.

Increased Focus on Literacy and the Language Demands of Content-Based Learning

Student literacy has become a major issue in American education. Standards-based reform and annual results on state assessments confirm that a high majority of American students struggle with the language demands of content learning in today's schools, particularly at the middle- and high-school levels. Adolescent literacy is emerging as a national concern, which is leading to an increased focus on the use of language in content areas and the language demands of learning tasks. The need to enhance adolescent literacy at the secondary level is not limited just to special needs students or English language learners, but exists for much of the student population (Moore, Bean, Birdyshaw, & Rycik, 1999).

The increasing focus on literacy in education reform may lead to a broader understanding of literacy issues for English language learners, especially at the middle- and high-school levels. Today, as students move through the upper grade levels, they face rapidly increasing literacy demands because of the expectations of new standards-based curricula. More reading and writing is required in solving problems and expressing ideas that reflect critical-thinking skills. Even in mathematics and science, students are expected to write explanations of their solutions and how they went about solving problems. They are expected to grapple with expository texts that are dense and full of new and difficult vocabulary, especially in math, science, and social studies (Allen, 2000).

In her comprehensive review of adolescent literacy research and practice, Meltzer (2001) underscores that if literacy skills are not firmly in place, are not fluent due to lack of practice, and are not continually scaffolded to improve with time, all but the most advanced readers and writers are placed at a disadvantage. She summarizes current research suggesting that teaching reading comprehension as a content-area learning strategy is a promising approach to enhancing adolescents' abilities to use reading and writing to learn content. However, practical knowledge of how to implement what have been identified as effective literacy strategies in secondary content-area classrooms is limited (National Reading Panel, 2000). Language will always be a central factor in determining the progress of English language learners in different content areas. Thus, the process of implementing learning standards with these students must address the impact of language skills on their ability to develop content-based proficiencies. Unless the language demands of content-area learning tasks are clearly understood, teachers will find it difficult to interpret the content-matter performance of English language learners because of the potential confounding of literacy skills with content knowledge.

A major challenge will be to improve language arts education for English language learners in light of emerging knowledge and understandings of literacy. This requires distinguishing between the goal of English language acquisition and the goal of developing complex literacy skills and understandings (Berman et al., 1995). A central question is how to guide English language learners into becoming competent readers and writers with complex literacy skills, a primary goal of today's standards-based English language arts curricula. Currently, more is known about second-language acquisition than how to translate that knowledge into effective school programs for English language learners. In addition, the knowledge base of how to guide students into becoming competent readers and writers across content areas is just emerging. The combined focus on standards, second-language acquisition, and literacy may lead to deeper understandings about the range of issues that must be addressed for English language learners. The orientation must shift from just moving language minority students into English classrooms to a developmental emphasis that combines what is known about language acquisition with emerging knowledge on best practices in developing student literacy.

USING PERFORMANCE-BASED ASSESSMENTS WITH ENGLISH LANGUAGE LEARNERS

Performance-based assessment is widely viewed as offering a means to measure student progress on learning standards and as being more responsive to diversity than traditional assessments. When teachers link standards to performance assessment, students must demonstrate their skills and abilities through a range of "performances," and new emphasis is placed on student work that involves higher-order thinking and complex problem solving. As noted previously, students are asked to apply the skills and competencies they have learned to "authentic" tasks that represent practical or "real-life" contexts. In performance assessment, teachers collect evidence of student learning through a variety of means such as oral presentations, exhibitions, student portfolios, experiments, cooperative group work, research projects, student journals, anecdotal records, notes from classroom observations, and teacher-student conferencing. In this way, performance assessments draw on a wider range of evidence than do other forms of assessment.

Performance assessments have the following key features:

- Measure student achievement against a continuum of agreed-upon standards of proficiency.
- Emphasize the importance of *context* through real-life tasks that are "authentic" to the learner.
- Focus on higher-order thinking processes and how students integrate information and skills in performing tasks.
- Require students to display what they know and are able to do by solving problems (performance tasks) of varying complexity, some of which involve multiple steps, several types of performance, and significant student time.
- Often involve group as well as individual performance on a task.

While performance assessments are promising in the flexibility they offer in accommodating diversity, not much research has been done on how performance-based assessments affect the education of students from diverse cultural, linguistic, and economic backgrounds. Some researchers have cautioned that there might be potential problems in using performance assessments fairly with culturally and linguistically diverse groups of students. However, the advantages of performance assessments for English language learners outweigh the concerns and are discussed next.

The use of performance assessments with English language learners is viewed with optimism because of their inherent flexibility and because they use multiple measures over time. Performance assessment allows teachers to document the broad-based process of learning, follow children's development, and create differentiated profiles of students' accomplishments. When performance assessments are used to support standards-based curricula, teachers and students often collaborate in the learning process.

Advantages of performance assessments for diverse learners:

- Promote active student learning and support instruction.
- Assist teachers to make instructional decisions by actively involving both students and teachers in the learning process.
- Minimize the likelihood of drawing conclusions from limited performance opportunities.
- Offer children from different backgrounds varied ways to display their knowledge and abilities.
- Provide information that can be used to form a profile of a student's individual strengths and weaknesses.
- Provide teachers with evidence to monitor student progress over time and to adjust instruction appropriately. (Meisels, Dorfman, & Steele, 1995)

Three major benefits of performance assessments for English language learners are that they (1) allow students to display proficiencies in a wide variety of ways; (2) allow more dynamic approaches to assessing student learning; and (3) allow developmental learning to be profiled over time.

Wide Range of Ways to Display Competencies

Performance assessments allow teachers to use varied methods to assess student progress. A range of activities provide teachers with a richer, more complete picture of what English language learners have learned in various content areas. Because performance assessments involve multiple ways of demonstrating proficiency, they invite students to draw on multiple intelligences and to display varied cognitive and communicative styles. As a result, these assessments provide a wider range of opportunities for English language learners to show what they know and can do in both language and content areas. Because they make greater cognitive demands on students than traditional tests do, performance tasks invite a fuller range of responses, provide a richer picture of what students have learned, and allow for the ongoing assessment of their higher-order thinking skills (Farr & Trumbull, 1997).

The flexibility of performance assessment allows teachers to vary the methods used to diagnose the learning of students whose cognitive and cultural styles may cause them to perform poorly on conventional tests. By offering a range of contexts—including opportunities to work alone, in pairs, or in groups—teachers can vary assessment settings to reflect cultural preferences and also to evaluate the impact of these contexts on particular students' progress. By examining how students solve tasks, teachers can better differentiate between learning problems caused by limited English skills and those caused by limited content knowledge. Because English language learners often experience academic difficulties or lack content understanding, examining their progress through a variety of learning tasks helps teachers better understand different learning styles, unique talents, and instructional needs. Using a range of assessment information to diagnose student learning also helps teachers modify or differentiate instruction more effectively.

Dynamic Assessment

When using performance assessments, an approach called *dynamic assessment* can help teachers differentiate between tasks that students can complete independently and tasks they can complete with varying levels of assistance. Dynamic assessment allows teachers to document the progress that ELL students are making with and without support. This approach assumes that assessment should be directed toward finding out what the student is capable of learning with the assistance of the teacher rather than just focusing on what the student already knows (Farr & Trumbull, 1997). Designed to reveal how a child learns, dynamic assessment procedures can provide students with a series of increasingly challenging tasks and offer varying levels of assistance to help students perform successfully. Proponents believe that dynamic assessment offers the opportunity to gain insights into how students learn, which instructional strategies facilitate learning, and which learners respond best to specific types of instruction. As a result, dynamic assessment can provide information about the effectiveness of specific instructional strategies.

Profile of Learning Over Time

Using multiple assessments at different points in time is particularly critical for students whose primary language is not English. Decisions about their abilities, proficiencies, and progress should never be made based on the results of a single test. English language learners need to show *how* they learn and *what* they have learned in ways that are comfortable for them and that reflect their communication capabilities. Offering them multiple opportunities to demonstrate proficiency in a content area may lead to more valid judgments about their progress and reveal productive "entry points" that build on their strengths and extend them into new areas of learning. It will also encourage them to draw on a wider range of thinking skills and allow for a deeper understanding of their approaches to learning situations and knowledge of content. Using multiple measures over time allows teachers to observe the development of students' thinking and organizational skills and create profiles of what students have learned. Teachers can also acquire more valid information about partial knowledge in a content area and the knowledge the student is developing (Farr & Trumbull, 1997).

HOW TO DETERMINE THE APPROPRIATENESS OF PERFORMANCE ASSESSMENTS

It is important for both content teachers and teachers who are knowledgeable about the cultural and linguistic backgrounds of students to work together in reviewing the appropriateness and fairness of performance assessments for students with varying levels of English proficiency. Research indicates that certain criteria, as shown in Figure 4.3, should be considered in determining the appropriateness of performance tasks for English language learners.

For performance assessments to be fair for all students, they must be modified to take into account how English language learners use language, and they must provide all students with a sufficient context for understanding and responding appropriately to the assessment task. If these considerations are not addressed, then English language learners will perform no better on performance assessments than they did on the traditional forms of assessment used in schools.

Resource A includes a comprehensive set of questions that can be used by teachers as guidelines for determining the appropriateness of performance assessments for English language learners. These questions address the relevant prior knowledge necessary to complete a performance task, language demands and cultural bias, and procedural bias and scoring criteria. By using these guidelines, teachers can work together to develop common understandings of how students' cultural backgrounds and communication styles may affect how they engage in learning tasks and whether performance assessments are free of bias.

Figure 4.3   Criteria for determining the appropriateness of assessments for English language learners

- The extent of English language learners' experiences with the concepts, knowledge, skills, and applications represented in the learning tasks.
- The language demands of tasks, particularly for tasks emphasizing higher-order thinking skills.
- Whether learning tasks include concepts, vocabulary, and activities that would not be familiar to students from a particular culture.
- The prior knowledge and understanding that English language learners need in order to make sense of learning tasks.
- Whether the standards for performance are known and familiar to English language learners, as well as the criteria for judging proficiency in a student exhibition or product.
- Whether English language learners will be able to connect their cultural backgrounds and experiences to what is expected in the learning task.
- Whether the assessment tasks are multidimensional in ways that accommodate different culturally based cognitive styles and modes of representing knowledge and understanding.
- Whether the English language learners have had experience with the format of the learning task or assessment.
- The types of accommodations that are needed for English language learners to have the same opportunities as other students to demonstrate what they know and can do.

Sources: Abedi, Lord, Hofstetter, & Baker, 2000; Abedi & Mirocha, 2001; Farr & Trumbull, 1997; Garcia, 1998; LaCelle-Peterson & Rivera, 1994; Neill, 1995

PROFESSIONAL DEVELOPMENT THAT SUPPORTS STANDARDS-BASED LEARNING

Professional development for teachers must be carefully integrated into each stage of a school's plan to implement high learning standards with culturally diverse student populations. To build an effective professional development program, schools must allot adequate time and resources for ongoing and sustained professional development activities, perhaps using both outside experts and peer training and support. Schools must also determine what teachers generally need to know and be able to do to implement standards-based instruction and assessment and where their teachers in particular need professional development. Implementing standards in schools with culturally diverse student populations requires a broad range of skills and requires teachers to make significant investments of time as they learn what standards mean for classroom practice. In addition to the range of skills needed to implement standards-based instruction, teachers also need opportunities to learn more about issues of language and culture and how they play out in the classroom.

Areas of professional development that will strengthen teachers' capacities to provide high quality instruction to English language learners are listed here.

Standards-Based Learning

- Implementing standards-based instruction and assessment with students who have varying levels of English proficiency.
- Using active teaching methods to engage students.
- Developing strategies for including all students in classroom discourse.
- Accommodating different learning styles.
- Using multiple forms of assessment to gather evidence of student proficiencies.
- Providing a variety of opportunities for students with varying levels of English proficiency to learn concepts over time.

The Cultural Context of Teaching

- Understanding how a teacher's own language and culture shape understanding of student performance.

- Understanding differences in the communication and cognitive styles of different cultures and how they may affect student participation in learning tasks.
- Developing learning tasks that connect to students' cultural backgrounds.
- Determining the prior knowledge necessary for a student to understand a learning task.
- Avoiding cultural bias in assessment, and creating and applying rubrics that are not culturally based.

Language and Learning

- Knowing about the factors that affect the development of a second language.
- Understanding the role of the primary language in second language learning.
- Using language in literacy development.
- Evaluating the language demands and cultural content of learning tasks.
- Understanding the requirements of academic language versus informal communication.
- Understanding how language structures and styles in written texts affect student understanding and comprehension.
- Knowing the types of accommodations that enhance the learning of English language learners.

To help schools and districts develop teacher knowledge about these activities, Resource B contains a Professional Development Self-Assessment and a Professional Development Planning Profile that can be used as tools for planning and developing ongoing professional development programs.

Emerging models of professional development aim to improve student learning by altering classroom practices in ways that benefit students. Thus, the focus of professional development has shifted toward an emphasis on student learning and the knowledge, skills, and attitudes required of teachers to improve student achievement (Darling-Hammond, 1997; Darling-Hammond & Sykes, 1999). The paradigm shift occurring in teacher development has teachers learning together and building on each other's wisdom and experience. This paradigm shift addresses the pervasive isolation that so many classroom teachers experience, emphasizing the importance of teachers being able to learn and communicate with colleagues in the place where it counts the most—the school. In many schools, teachers with expertise in working with English language learners are often isolated from mainstream teachers who would benefit from their expertise, and mainstream teachers without sufficient professional development have English language learners placed in their classrooms (Teemant, Bernhardt, Rodriquez-Munoz, & Aiello, 2000).

New approaches will have teachers collaborating with each other through ongoing, inquiry-based learning opportunities that help them develop deeper understanding of the teaching/learning process in their own contexts. This form of professional development is job embedded, with teachers studying teaching and learning processes through study groups, observing peers, and becoming involved in curriculum improvement processes. The professional development process (1) is results oriented; (2) focuses teacher development around raising student achievement for highly diverse student populations; (3) engages teachers actively in continuous inquiry-based learning; (4) occurs within the context of the school, where new practices can be tried and refined; (5) creates opportunities for shared understanding among colleagues; and (6) enhances teacher leaders' capacities to sustain instructional reform.

CHAPTER FIVE

Achieving the Vision of Higher Standards for All

This book has discussed major trends that have shifted education policy and are having a widespread impact on American schooling. These trends reflect legislative mandates that are creating new expectations for accountability, new knowledge about the process of learning, new forms of assessment, and a rapid increase in the English language learner population in schools. The transformation of the American education system over the past decade and the emergence of standards-based state assessments are stimulating a new vision of K–12 education and the policies and practices necessary to ensure both equity and excellence for all students.

This final chapter summarizes some of the policy and practice implications of education reform at both state and school levels; it also presents policy and practice guidelines on major issues that must be addressed, reflecting the research and knowledge base described in previous chapters.

STATE POLICIES AND PRACTICES THAT SUPPORT EQUITABLE ASSESSMENT FOR ENGLISH LANGUAGE LEARNERS

Research and practice suggest that the following principles and approaches should guide state-level policies that govern the large-scale assessment of English language learners.

Provide leadership that helps educators and the public understand and accept new assumptions about the purpose of standards-based state assessments

Educators and the public continue to need help in accepting the value system underlying new standards-based assessments and the mandate that all students, including students with limited English proficiency, are expected to demonstrate proficiency. The value system underlying a "ranking and comparing" model of assessment has had a powerful influence on the thinking of educators and the public at large. Policymakers and educational leaders still have to build support for the belief that all students are capable of learning and achieving at high levels, and that the primary purpose of assessment systems is to guide and measure student progress toward desired standards of excellence that are the same for all students.

Ensure that assessment policies address the dual goals of excellence and equity in the nation's schools

It is still not known how new assessments will affect students in schools with the least supportive environments and students from non-mainstream backgrounds. Policymakers and educational leaders must still give attention to the unintended consequences that may result from the use of new assessments, and they must ensure fairness and lack of cultural bias in high-stakes assessments. Assessment results are not valid when students' abilities have not been judged fairly because of the inappropriateness or bias of the assessment. Policies must ensure that tests are used appropriately for all students.

Choose assessment content that is appropriate for the diverse populations taking the test

Those who develop assessment tests should consider both the diverse cultural backgrounds represented in a student population and the amount of knowledge that these students need about mainstream culture in order to understand and respond to an assessment item or performance task. Because many English language learners draw on life experiences that differ from those who develop assessments, these students often respond to performance assessments in unanticipated ways.

Include English language learners in the field-test of state assessments to ensure validity

State assessments must be field tested with a student sample that is representative of the test population. Making inferences about the competencies of English language learners from assessments that have been validated with monolingual English-speaking students only constitutes an invalid use of assessment data. Only assessments that have included English language learners in their field-test population sample will be valid for use with these students.

Establish scoring criteria appropriate for evaluating the work of English language learners and properly train those who score assessments

Assessment scoring criteria must make it possible to differentiate the content-area knowledge, skills, and abilities being tested from the linguistic skill with which student responses are expressed. Otherwise English language learners will be penalized inappropriately for lacking English language skills. In the case of performance assessments, individuals who are knowledgeable about the cultural and linguistic characteristics of the students being assessed should participate in the development of rubrics for scoring student work. Furthermore, assessment personnel who score the responses of English language learners must be carefully selected and trained.

Document the use of accommodations that maximize the inclusion of English language learners in state assessments

States need to collect data documenting how various accommodations are used and how effective they are inpromoting the participation of English language learner students in statewide assessments. Accommodations do not work equally well for all English language learners because of wide variations in English language proficiency. Accommodations may make a positive difference for English language learners who already are fairly proficient in English, but, for those students who have very little proficiency in English, accommodations may not make enough of a difference to enable them to perform at high level.

The issue of consistency or comparability of taking a test with and without accommodations will not be resolved easily from a technical standpoint. Because of this, it has been suggested that the assessment results of students who take an assessment without accommodations should be separated from those students who take the assessment with accommodations. The use of alternative assessment strategies and accommodations requires more research, analysis, and evaluation of assessment practices to determine their comparability to the assessments used to measure the progress of fluent English speakers.

Ensure that translated assessments are equivalent to the English version of the assessment

Careful procedures must be followed to ensure that translated versions of state assessments measure the same underlying concepts and competencies as the English versions.

Translated test items may convey substantially different meanings than the original English item, because concepts and terminology do not always have perfect equivalents in different languages. Because of the difficulties involved in direct translation of test items, back translation has become a highly recommended procedure. The process involves translation into a second language and then translation back into English. Through a series of at least three back translations, items are matched and modified to avoid inadvertent discrepancies in the translated assessment.

Disaggregate assessment data to monitor the achievement of English language learners

Statewide assessment results should be disaggregated to determine how English language learners are performing as a group. The reporting of disaggregated data at state and district levels will allow for an understanding of the academic development and achievement trends of English language learners and enable local educators to make more meaningful judgments about the effectiveness of instructional programs. In addition, data collected in state accountability assessments should include background information on English language learners such as their primary language and the length of time they have received content instruction in English and instruction in English as a second language.

SCHOOL POLICIES AND PRACTICES THAT SUPPORT HIGH STANDARDS FOR ENGLISH LANGUAGE LEARNERS

Translating the mission of "high standards for all" into reality requires policies and practices that provide clear direction and guidance for instruction and assessment. School policies communicate the school's beliefs about the quality of education that should be offered to all students; they also send strong messages about the school's commitment to ensuring fairness and equity in instructional practice. High expectations should be set for all students, and all students should have high quality instruction and access to the resources necessary for learning. Assessment measures should be unbiased, and their results used appropriately. Lessons learned from those schools that have been successful in providing effective learning environments for English language learners have highlighted several important practices:

- A comprehensive, schoolwide vision provided the essential foundation for developing a high quality educational program for English language learners.
- A schoolwide approach was used to restructure the learning environment and uses of instructional time to improve the academic achievement of English language learners.
- Effective language development strategies were implemented to achieve two goals—that English language learners would achieve English fluency and also master the content of the core curriculum provided to all students.
- High quality learning environments for English language learners involved curricular strategies that engaged students in meaningful, in-depth learning across content areas led by trained and qualified staff.
- Innovative instructional strategies were used with English language learners emphasizing collaboration and hands-on activities to actively engage them in the learning process. (Berman et al., 1995)

Schoolwide policies and practices that are key to supporting a high quality education in culturally and linguistically diverse schools are shown in Figure 5.1. A practical tool for assessing a school's status against these desired policies and practices can be found in Resource C.

Figure 5.1   School policies and practices that support high quality learning in culturally diverse schools

---

Policies and Practices

- There is a schoolwide vision of high expectations for all students.
- The curriculum offered to all students is based on the same standards for what students should know and be able to do.
- All students are provided with opportunities to achieve at high levels.
- All students are provided with equitable and adequate learning resources and high quality instruction.
- The learning environment and uses of instructional time have been organized to enhance learning for all students.
- Time and resources are allocated for the ongoing professional development and teacher collaboration necessary to support high quality teaching with diverse student populations.
- School policies support the appropriate use of accommodations to ensure all students have equal opportunities to develop and demonstrate essential proficiencies.
- There is schoolwide understanding of the varied purposes and uses of different types of assessments and the measures that are appropriate.
- Emphasis is on equity and fairness in assessment for all students and clear policies to help teachers avoid bias in the use or interpretation of assessments.
- All assessments are used for the primary purpose of improving student learning; that is, assessments are not used to place students in limiting programs or to inhibit educational opportunities.

Research and practice suggest the following principles and approaches as guidelines for establishing school policies and practices that support high quality learning for English language learners.

Provide English language learners with instruction
that will enable them to develop higher-order proficiencies

English language learners must have adequate opportunities to develop proficiencies based on high learning standards. This means ensuring that they have been exposed to challenging learning situations and the full range of desired educational outcomes. They should be thoroughly grounded in what is expected of them, provided opportunities to learn the content being assessed, and taught in ways that will enable them to respond to the more complex and cognitively demanding tasks of performance assessments. Most important, they must have equitable access to the educational resources and high quality teachers that will support them in learning and achieving at high levels.

Encourage teachers of English language learners to make connections between academic tasks and the home cultures of students

Far more attention must be given to connecting instructional goals, methods, and materials to students' cultural experiences and to the range of learning styles students bring to the classroom. This does not mean that learning should be limited to topics that relate to the experiences students bring to school, but rather that these experiences serve as starting points for making knowledge meaningful. The challenge is to make effective instructional use of the personal and cultural knowledge of students while at the same time helping them reach beyond their cultural boundaries.

Give English language learners additional
time and support when they are learning classroom
uses of language that are unfamiliar to them

The organization of classroom instruction should allow sufficient time for English language learners to develop their understanding of how to use language in learning situations. English language learners who use patterns of language at home that are different than those commonly used in mainstream classrooms should be given instructional support and extra time to expand their repertoire of language use.

Use authentic assessments that draw on English language learners' real-life situations

Authentic assessments connected to real-life situations will help English language learners understand and apply essential concepts, knowledge, and skills. When developing assessments for linguistically and culturally diverse student populations, teachers should consider how student life experiences will affect responses to assessments. English language learners will learn more effectively if assessment tasks connect to their frame of reference and their personal experiences. Teachers who wish to develop authentic and meaningful assessments for English language learners should draw on English language learners' home and community experiences as strengths to be integrated more effectively into instruction.

Use multiple assessment strategies so English language learners have a wide range of options when showing what they know and can do

School policies should emphasize the use of a variety of assessments to monitor student learning. This is especially critical for English language learners who need to demonstrate their progress in both language and academic areas over time. They must be given multiple opportunities to show how they learn and to demonstrate what they have learned in ways that are comfortable for them and reflect their communication capabilities. Flexibility in assessment is important to accommodating students' learning styles, aptitudes, and interests, and will produce more meaningful results. Latitude should also be given in the time allowed to complete assessment tasks, allowing English language learners time to experiment, draft, reflect, and revise their work. Allowing English language learners to demonstrate their competence in a variety of ways will yield a deeper understanding of their approach to learning situations, their knowledge of content, and their thinking skills. The use of varied strategies will be important for teachers as well because it will enhance their ability to determine English language learners' progress across a wider range of learning areas, and enrich their awareness of cultural differences in how their students approach learning.

Establish scoring criteria for classroom performance assessments that are appropriate for English language learners

Because performance assessments require teachers to apply clearly defined criteria when determining the level of proficiency a student has demonstrated in responding to a task, special attention must be given to whether scoring criteria provide the basis for a fair evaluation of the responses of English language learners. In developing scoring rubrics, involve district and school staff who are knowledgeable about the linguistic and cultural characteristics of students and who understand how language and culture influence learning. The performance criteria used to assess English language learners are likely to be unreliable if they are developed by staff who hold views of quality performance that conflict with the understanding of specialists who are most knowledgeable about teaching linguistically and culturally diverse children. It is especially important that the role of language be explicitly considered when developing scoring criteria so that English language learners are not penalized inappropriately for lacking English language skills. Content-area performance assessments should be scored based on the knowledge, skills, and abilities being assessed, not on the quality of the language in which the response is expressed.

The background and expertise of scorers can affect an assessment's fairness and validity, and staff must have adequate expertise and training in order to score the performance responses of English language learners fairly. Teaching staff and specialists can benefit from working as a team in scoring the work of English language learners because, by doing so, they can deepen their understanding of the relationships between performance standards and effective instructional strategies for English language learners.

Develop clear guidelines for interpreting assessment results so that English language learners are not placed inappropriately in special education classes

Guidelines for selecting assessment tools for determining the need for special education services must go beyond satisfying the legal requirements for testing students to also include an assessment of students' English proficiency and second language development. Assessments need to distinguish between English language learners who are performing unsatisfactorily in school because of limited exposure to English and children who demonstrate communication disorders and need special education intervention.

Make significant investments in professional development

Preparing teachers to use recognized best practices when educating diverse student populations requires significant investments in professional development. Few teachers are skilled in research-based approaches to learning. Because these practices have not yet spread to most of the nation's schools, professional development is a key to advancing improvements in classroom instruction. Professional development for teachers should be carefully integrated into each stage of a school's plan to implement high learning standards with culturally diverse student populations. To build an effective professional development program, schools must allot adequate time and resources for ongoing and sustained professional development activities, perhaps using both outside experts and peer training and support. Schools must also determine what teachers generally need to know and be able to do to implement standards-based instruction and assessment with diverse learners, and the areas where teachers need particular help.

For teachers to support the use of alternative assessments with English language learners, they must be proficient not only in subject matter knowledge and current theories of how students learn, but also in knowledge of how language and culture influence student learning and performance. Professional development plans should acknowledge that the requirements of second language development add another dimension to the instructional decisions teachers have to make, and they should call for strategies that specifically meet the needs of students who are developing second language proficiency. Schools should also address the isolation of classroom teachers from ESL/bilingual teachers who could provide expertise on strategies that support language development and learning for students not fully proficient in English. Teachers will need sustained and in-depth professional development as they learn to evaluate the language demands and cultural content of instructional activities and develop an understanding of the communication styles and patterns of their students' cultures. They will need opportunities to learn more about language and culture and how they affect the classroom, and be able to develop deeper knowledge about particular cultural communities.

ACHIEVING THE VISION OF HIGH STANDARDS FOR ALL

The mission of "high standards for all" has created a new policy perspective that is shaping how education is conducted in every classroom across America. Basing state assessments on performance standards has challenged policies that dominated public schools for more than a half century. "Assessment for ranking" has been exchanged for "assessment to improve student learning." By changing assessment *content* (to knowledge and skills that are based on standards) and *form* (to tasks that invite complex performances), new approaches to assessment significantly alter how students demonstrate what they know and can do. This new policy perspective requires educators and the public to accept that, instead of comparing students to each other, it is more important to consider the progress of students in developing standards-based proficiencies.

Because "high standards for all students" is such a new vision, American education must focus attention on the kinds of issues identified in this book. The quality of education that was offered to "the best and the brightest" is now the quality of education that must be available to all. Standards-based learning requires teachers to develop new skills and see their role in new ways. They must be able to build instruction around performance tasks, organize learning around holistic concepts, guide student inquiry, provide a variety of opportunities for students to explore concepts and problem situations over time, use multiple forms of assessment to gather evidence of student proficiencies, and make informed judgments about student progress. American education will need highly skilled teachers to implement these strategies and to offer a range of learning opportunities that connect to different learning styles. The emphasis on high standards will also cause a new focus on the quality of learning environments and the range of resources necessary to support high academic achievement for learners who come from diverse cultural and linguistic backgrounds.

Finally, as the results from new standards-based assessments are released, communities will need to recognize that these assessments represent some areas of knowledge and skills that traditionally were not taught to the general student population in most schools, and particularly not to English language learners. Initial test scores will be important benchmarks for examining the extent to which various segments of our student populations have been exposed to essential teachings in today's world. These early results are an important foundation for identifying where current curriculum and practice promotes high standards of learning for all students, and where curriculum improvement and professional development are clearly necessary if equity in learning is to be achieved.

Resource A

Guiding Questions for Determining the Appropriateness of Learning Tasks in Performance Assessments for English Language Learners

It is important for both content teachers and teachers who are knowledgeable about the cultural and linguistic backgrounds of students to work together in reviewing the appropriateness and fairness of the learning tasks used in performance assessments for culturally and linguistically diverse students. The questions below can be used as guidelines for conducting such a review.

Relevant Prior Knowledge

- What common experiences and understandings are required of students to make sense of the assessment task and productively undertake its solution?
- Will students be able to connect their cultural background and their experiences to what is expected in the assessment task?
- What is the extent of students' prior experiences with the concepts, knowledge, skills, and applications represented in the assessment?

- Is there reason to believe that students from different cultural groups may not be motivated by the topics covered in the task?
- Are the criteria for judging student performance known and familiar to students from diverse cultural backgrounds; do all students understand the processes and products of learning that represent high-quality work in the assessment task?

Language Demands and Cultural Bias

- Has consideration been given to the language demands of the learning task for students from diverse language backgrounds, particularly for tasks emphasizing higher-order thinking skills?
- If the focus of the task is not language facility, are there alternative ways for students with limited English proficiency to display their understanding?
- Does the assessment task include concepts, vocabulary, and activities that would not be familiar to students from a particular culture?
- Are the limited number of topics used in the performance assessment relevant to a broad number of students?
- Are assessment tasks multidimensional in ways that allow students from diverse cultural backgrounds to demonstrate their understanding?
- What accommodations would be necessary to give students with limited English proficiency the same opportunity available to monolingual students to demonstrate what they know and can do?

Procedural Bias and Scoring Criteria

- Do the assessment tasks unduly penalize students for whom the types of activities necessary in completing the task may be unfamiliar?

- Do the time limits deprive students with limited English language proficiency of the amount of time they need to complete an assessment task?
- Do the criteria used to judge student performance favor particular cultural orientations?
- What is the role of language in the scoring criteria? Specifically, do the scoring criteria for content-area assessments focus on the knowledge, skills, and abilities being tested, and not on the quality of the language in which the response is expressed? Would students be placed at a disadvantage if they lacked English language skills?
- Do the teachers who will assess student performance include staff who are sufficiently familiar with students' cultural and linguistic backgrounds to make appropriate interpretations of student performances? Are the raters who score students' work trained to recognize and score the performance of students from varied cultural and linguistic backgrounds? Do raters include educators from the same linguistic and cultural backgrounds as the students? (Baker, 1997; Baker & O'Neil, 1995; Estrin & Nelson-Barber, 1995; Farr & Trumbull, 1997; Garcia & Pearson, 1994; LaCelle-Peterson & Rivera, 1994; Lachat, 1999a; Neill, 1995; Rivera & Vincent, 1996)

A Tool for Determining the Appropriateness of Learning Tasks in Performance Assessments for English Language Learners

This tool can be used by a team to review the appropriateness of performance tasks for English language learners. Team members should review the tasks and record their comments.

Relevant Prior Knowledge	*Comments of Review Team Members on Fairness of Performance Tasks in Terms of Relevant Prior Knowledge*
• What common experiences and understandings are required of students to make sense of the assessment task and productively undertake its solution?	
• Will students be able to connect their cultural background and experiences to what is expected in the assessment task?	
• What is the extent of students' prior experiences with the concepts, knowledge, skills, and applications represented in the assessment task?	
• Is there reason to believe that students from different cultural groups may not be motivated by the topics covered in the task?	
• Are the criteria for judging student performance known and familiar to culturally diverse students; do the students understand the processes and products of learning that represent high-quality work in the assessment task?	

Language Demands and Cultural Bias	*Comments of Review Team Members on Fairness of Performance Tasks in Terms of Language Demands and Cultural Bias*
• Has consideration been given to the language demands of the learning task for students from diverse language backgrounds, particularly for tasks emphasizing higher-order thinking skills?	
• If the focus of the task is not language facility, are there alternative ways for students with limited English proficiency to display their understanding?	
• Does the assessment task include concepts, vocabulary, and activities that would not be familiar to students from a particular culture?	
• Are the limited number of topics used in the performance assessment relevant to a broad number of students?	
• Are assessment tasks multidimensional in ways that allow students from diverse language backgrounds to demonstrate their understanding?	
• What accommodations would be necessary to give students with limited English proficiency the same opportunity available to monolingual students to demonstrate what they know and can do?	

Procedural Bias and Scoring Criteria	*Comments of Review Team Members on Fairness of Performance Tasks in Terms of Procedural Bias and Scoring Criteria*
• Do the assessment tasks unduly penalize students for whom the types of activities necessary in completing the task may be unfamiliar?	
• Do the time limits deprive students with limited English language proficiency of the amount of time they need to complete an assessment task?	
• Do the criteria used to judge student performance favor particular cultural orientations?	
• What is the role of language in the scoring criteria? Specifically, do the scoring criteria for content-area assessments focus on the knowledge, skills, and abilities being tested, and not on the quality of the language in which the response is expressed? Would students be placed at a disadvantage if they lacked English language skills?	
• Do the teachers who will assess student performance include staff who are sufficiently familiar with students' cultural and linguistic backgrounds to make appropriate interpretations of student performances?	
• Are the raters who score students' work trained to recognize and score the performance of students from varied cultural and linguistic backgrounds? Do raters include educators from the same linguistic and cultural backgrounds as the students?	

Resource B

Professional Development That Supports the Learning and Achievement of English Language Learners

Teachers can benefit from concrete professional development opportunities tied directly to aspects of instruction and assessment that effectively support the learning and achievement of English language learners. This appendix includes a Professional Development Self-Assessment Survey and a Professional Development Planning Profile that can be used as tools for planning and developing a proficiency-based professional development program. They identify some of the teacher proficiencies (what teachers must know and be able to do) that are essential to effectively implementing high quality instruction and assessment with culturally and linguistically diverse learners.

The Professional Development Self-Assessment Survey is a tool that allows teachers to indicate their professional development priorities in areas that are essential to supporting the learning and achievement of English language learners. Teachers use a four-point scale, with 1 being the lowest and 4 being the highest, to rate the importance of each professional development area in helping them to work more effectively with their students. They are also asked to indicate areas where they feel they could serve as a resource in assisting other teachers in the school to develop deeper understandings and skills.

The results of this self-assessment can be used to develop a proficiency-based professional development program for teachers around specific aspects of instruction and assessment for English language learners.

The Professional Development Planning Profile is a tool for summarizing the results of the Professional Development Self-Assessment Survey and for engaging a school team in collaboratively developing a plan for professional development and defining criteria for assessing the effectiveness of the professional development opportunities provided. The planning process itself affords teachers and administrators an important opportunity to communicate about various areas of proficiency and how best to engage teachers in an ongoing process of development.

Professional Development
Self-Assessment Survey Supporting the Learning
and Achievement of English Language Learners

This Professional Development Self-Assessment Survey identifies several areas of instruction and assessment that are essential to supporting the learning and achievement of English language learners. It allows you to identify your priorities for professional development in these areas. Use the four-point scale, with 1 being the lowest and 4 being the highest, to rate the importance of each area of professional development in helping you work more effectively with culturally and linguistically diverse students. Also, please indicate areas where you feel you could serve as a resource in assisting other teachers in the school to develop deeper understandings and skills.

Professional Development Self-Assessment Survey

Areas of Professional Development	Circle a number from 1 to 4, rating its importance to you in professional development.				I could help other teachers in this area. (✓)
	Low Need			*High Need*	
Standards-Based Learning					
1. Implementing standards-based instruction with students who have varying levels of English proficiency.	1	2	3	4	☐
2. Using active teaching methods to engage English language learners.	1	2	3	4	☐
3. Using different strategies for including all students in classroom discourse.	1	2	3	4	☐
4. Accommodating different learning styles.	1	2	3	4	☐
5. Using multiple forms of assessment to gather evidence of student proficiencies.	1	2	3	4	☐
6. Providing a variety of opportunities for students with varying levels of English proficiency to learn concepts over time.	1	2	3	4	☐
The Cultural Context of Teaching					
7. Understanding how a teacher's own language and culture shape understanding of student performance.	1	2	3	4	☐
8. Understanding differences in the communication and cognitive styles of different cultures and how they may affect student participation in learning tasks.	1	2	3	4	☐

(Continued)

(Continued)

Areas of Professional Development	Circle a number from 1 to 4, rating its importance to you in professional development.				I could help other teachers in this area. (✓)
	Low Need		High Need		
9. Developing learning tasks that connect to students' cultural backgrounds.	1	2	3	4	☐
10. Determining the prior knowledge necessary for a student to understand a learning task.	1	2	3	4	☐
11. Avoiding cultural bias in assessment: creating and applying rubrics that are not culturally based.	1	2	3	4	☐
Learning and Language					
12. Understanding the factors that affect the development of a second language.	1	2	3	4	☐
13. Knowing the role of the primary language in second language learning.	1	2	3	4	☐
14. Using language in literacy development.	1	2	3	4	☐
15. Evaluating the language demands and cultural content of learning tasks.	1	2	3	4	☐
16. Understanding the requirements of academic language versus informal communication.	1	2	3	4	☐
17. Understanding how language structures and styles in written texts affect student understanding and comprehension.	1	2	3	4	☐
18. Knowing the types of accommodations that enhance the learning of English language learners.	1	2	3	4	☐

Professional Development Planning Profile

Areas of Professional Development	Summary of Teacher Ratings of Importance: (1 = low to 4 = high) Indicate number of teachers that checked each rating.				Number of teachers available to assist others in each area.
	Low 1	2	3	High 4	
Standards-Based Learning					
1. Implementing standards-based instruction with students who have varying levels of English proficiency.	—	—	—	—	——
2. Using active teaching methods to engage English language learners.	—	—	—	—	——
3. Using different strategies for including all students in classroom discourse.	—	—	—	—	——
4. Accommodating different learning styles.	—	—	—	—	——
5. Using multiple forms of assessment to gather evidence of student proficiencies.	—	—	—	—	——
6. Providing a variety of opportunities for students with varying levels of English proficiency to learn concepts over time.	—	—	—	—	——
The Cultural Context of Teaching					
7. Understanding how a teacher's own language and culture shape understanding of student performance.	—	—	—	—	——
8. Understanding differences in the communication and cognitive styles of different cultures and how they may affect student participation in learning tasks.	—	—	—	—	——

(Continued)

Areas of Professional Development	Summary of Teacher Ratings of Importance: (1=low to 4=high) Indicate number of teachers that checked each rating.				Number of teachers available to assist others in each area.
	Low 1	2	3	High 4	
9. Developing learning tasks that connect to students' cultural backgrounds.	—	—	—	—	—
10. Determining the prior knowledge necessary for a student to understand a learning task.	—	—	—	—	—
11. Avoiding cultural bias in assessment: creating and applying rubrics that are not culturally based.	—	—	—	—	—
Language and Learning					
12. Understanding the factors that affect the development of a second language.	—	—	—	—	—
13. Knowing the role of the primary language in second language learning.	—	—	—	—	—
14. Using language in literacy development.	—	—	—	—	—
15. Evaluating the language demands and cultural content of learning tasks.	—	—	—	—	—
16. Understanding the requirements of academic language versus informal communication.	—	—	—	—	—
17. Understanding how language structures and styles in written texts affect student understanding and comprehension.	—	—	—	—	—
18. Knowing the types of accommodations that enhance the learning of English language learners.	—	—	—	—	—

Example: Professional Development Planning Profile

Area of Proficiency	
Use active teaching methods to engage English language learners.	
Plan for Addressing Proficiency Area	*Plan for Evaluating the Effectiveness of Professional Development*
Describe the combination of professional development activities that will be used to develop teacher proficiency in this area. These might include the use of an outside consultant for training, classroom demonstration, and facilitation, as well as peer training and demonstration.	What quality and performance criteria should be used to assess the effectiveness of professional development activities for increasing teacher proficiency?

Example: Professional Development Planning Profile

Area of Proficiency	
Understand differences in the communication and cognitive styles of different cultures and how they may affect student participation in learning tasks.	
Plan for Addressing Proficiency Area	*Plan for Evaluating the Effectiveness of Professional Development*
Describe the combination of professional development activities that will be used to develop teacher proficiency in this area. These might include the use of an outside consultant for training, classroom demonstration, and facilitation, as well as peer training and demonstration.	What quality and performance criteria should be used to assess the effectiveness of professional development activities for increasing teacher proficiency?

Resource C

Policies and Practices That Support
the Learning and Achievement
of English Language Learners

The research literature has identified policies and practices that reflect a high-standards orientation to learning and that result in learning environments that support and enhance high quality instruction and assessment for all students, including English language learners. These indicators of a high-performing school include schoolwide policies and practices as well as classroom practices. They are identified below, followed by a Policy and Practice Self-Assessment Survey that school staff can use to assess their school's status against these indicators.

POLICIES AND PRACTICES

Schoolwide Policies and Practices

1. The curriculum offered to *all* students is based on high standards for what students should know and be able to do.

2. All students have opportunities to develop higher-order proficiencies.

3. All students are provided with high-quality learning resources and instruction.

4. The schedule allows flexible uses of time to support and enhance learning.

5. The physical environment of the school has been structured to support and enhance learning.

6. Decisions about resource allocation, scheduling, and staffing are *data driven*, with a central focus on fostering high achievement and success for all learners in the school.

7. Professional development, focusing on the teacher knowledge and skills essential to preparing diverse learners to achieve at high levels, is ongoing.

8. Emphasis is on shared responsibility and accountability for student learning and student success.

9. There are coordinated efforts to improve the achievement of low-performing students.

10. Procedures determine the appropriateness of various assessments for students with different levels of language proficiency.

11. Guidelines are in place for using accommodations to enhance the learning of English language learners.

12. Guidelines are in place to help school staff interpret and use multiple types of student performance data to monitor student progress and program effectiveness.

13. Assessment results are used by school staff to improve instruction and student learning.

Classroom Practices

1. Instruction is organized around clear performance standards—students know what is expected of them.

2. Classroom and extra time are structured to ensure that all students meet or exceed the standards.

3. Teachers implement strategies to involve all students in classroom discussion.

4. Different modes of learning are accommodated to help all students achieve the standards.

5. The emphasis is on real-world tasks requiring students to question, explore, research, make decisions, and communicate their findings.

6. A variety of grouping strategies are used to enhance student learning—students have opportunities to collaborate with each other and share responsibility for completing learning tasks.

7. Teachers draw upon the home and community experiences of students from diverse cultural backgrounds.

8. Assessment is integrated with instruction and directly linked to performance expectations.

9. Multiple assessment measures are used, offering a variety of ways for students to demonstrate what they know and can do.

10. Classroom assessments and scoring rubrics are free of cultural bias and do not penalize students with varying levels of English proficiency.

11. Students have ongoing opportunities to self-assess their work based on standards of performance.

12. Frequent feedback, reflecting the learning standards and related rubrics, is provided to students.

POLICIES AND PRACTICES THAT SUPPORT THE LEARNING AND ACHIEVEMENT OF ENGLISH LANGUAGE LEARNERS

Schoolwide Policies and Practices

Use this form to assess the status of the following schoolwide policies and practices in your school—whether they (1) need to be developed, (2) are in development, (3) need improvement, or (4) are in place.

	Status of Policy/Practice			
	Circle a number from 1 to 4 rating the status of the following schoolwide policies and practices in your school.			
Schoolwide Policies and Practices	Needs to Be Developed	In Development	Needs Improvement	In Place
1. The curriculum offered to *all* students is based on high standards for what students should know and be able to do.	1	2	3	4
2. All students have opportunities to develop higher-order proficiencies.	1	2	3	4
3. All students are provided with high-quality learning resources and instruction.	1	2	3	4
4. The schedule allows flexible use of time to support and enhance learning.	1	2	3	4
5. The physical environment of the school has been structured to support and enhance learning.	1	2	3	4
6. Decisions about resource allocation, scheduling, and staffing are *data driven*, with a central focus on fostering high achievement and success for all learners in the school.	1	2	3	4
7. Professional development, focusing on the teacher knowledge and skills essential to preparing diverse learners to achieve at high levels, is ongoing.	1	2	3	4

	Status of Policy/Practice			
	Circle a number from 1 to 4 rating the status of the following schoolwide policies and practices in your school.			
Schoolwide Policies and Practices	*Needs to Be Developed*	*In Development*	*Needs Improvement*	*In Place*
8. Emphasis is on shared responsibility and accountability for student learning and student success.	1	2	3	4
9. There are coordinated efforts to improve the achievement of low-performing students.	1	2	3	4
10. Procedures determine the appropriateness of various assessments for students with different levels of language proficiency.	1	2	3	4
11. Guidelines are in place for using accommodations to enhance the learning of English language learners.	1	2	3	4
12. Guidelines are in place to help school staff interpret and use multiple types of student performance data to monitor student progress and program effectiveness.	1	2	3	4
13. Assessment results are used by school staff to improve instruction and student learning.	1	2	3	4

Classroom Practices

Use this form to indicate the extent to which the following classroom practices are implemented in your school: (1) Not at All, (2) Small Extent, (3) Moderate Extent, or (4) A Great Extent.

| | Extent of Implementation | | | |
| | Circle a number from 1 to 4 rating the extent to which the following classroom practices are implemented in your school. | | | |
Classroom Practices	*Not at All*	*Small Extent*	*Moderate Extent*	*A Great Extent*
1. Instruction is organized around clear performance standards—students know what is expected of them.	1	2	3	4
2. Classroom and extra time are structured to ensure that all students meet or exceed the standards.	1	2	3	4
3. Teachers implement strategies to involve all students in classroom discussion.	1	2	3	4
4. Different modes of learning are accommodated to help all students achieve the standards.	1	2	3	4
5. Emphasis is on real-world tasks requiring students to question, explore, research, make decisions, and communicate their findings.	1	2	3	4
6. A variety of grouping strategies are used to enhance student learning—students have opportunities to collaborate	1	2	3	4

	Extent of Implementation			
	Circle a number from 1 to 4 rating the extent to which the following classroom practices are implemented in your school.			
Classroom Practices	*Not at All*	*Small Extent*	*Moderate Extent*	*A Great Extent*
with each other and share responsibility for completing learning tasks.				
7. Teachers draw upon the home and community experiences of students from diverse cultural backgrounds.	1	2	3	4
8. Assessment is integrated with instruction and directly linked to performance expectations.	1	2	3	4
9. Multiple assessment measures are used that offer a variety of ways for students to demonstrate what they know and can do.	1	2	3	4
10. Classroom assessments and scoring rubrics are free of cultural bias and do not penalize students with varying levels of English proficiency.	1	2	3	4
11. Students have ongoing opportunities to self-assess their work based on standards of performance.	1	2	3	4
12. Frequent feedback, reflecting the learning standards and related rubrics, is provided.	1	2	3	4

References

Abedi, J., Leon, S., & Mirocha, J. (2001). *Impact of students' language background on standardized achievement test results: Analyses of extant data*. Los Angeles: University of California, National Center for Research on Evaluation, Standards, and Student Testing (CRESST).

Abedi, J., Lord, C., Hofstetter, C., & Baker, E. (2000). Impact of accommodation strategies on English language learners' test performance. *Educational Measurement: Issues and Practice, 19*(3), 16–26.

Allen, J. (2000). *Yellow brick roads: Shared and guided paths to independent reading*. Portland, ME: Stenhouse.

American Education Research Association, American Psychological Association, & National Council of Measurement in Education. (1999). *Standards for educational & psychological testing*. Washington, DC: American Psychological Association.

American Federation of Teachers. (1999). *Making standards matter: 1996*. Washington, DC: Author.

Anderson, N. E., Jenkins, F. F., & Miller, K. E. (1996). *NAEP inclusion criteria and testing accommodations: Findings from the NAEP 1995 field test in mathematics*. Washington, DC: Educational Testing Service.

August, D., & Hakuta, K. (Eds.). (1997). *Improving schooling for language-minority children: A research agenda*. Washington, DC: National Academy Press.

August, D., & McArthur, E. (1996). *Proceedings of the conference on inclusion guidelines and accommodations for limited English proficient students in the national assessment of educational progress, December 5–6, 1994*. Washington, DC: U.S. Department of Education.

August, D., & Pease-Alvarez, L. (1996). *Attributes of effective programs and classrooms serving English language learners*. Washington, DC: The National Center for Research on Cultural Diversity and Second Language Learning.

Baker, E. L. (1997, Autumn). Model-based performance assessment. *Theory Into Practice, 36*(4), 247–254.

Baker, E. L., & Linn, R. L. (2002). Validity issues for accountability systems. *CSE Technical Report 585.* Los Angeles, CA: University of California, National Center for Research on Evaluation, Standards, and Student Testing (CRESST).

Baker, E., & O'Neil, H. (1995). Diversity, assessment, and equity in educational reform. In M. Nettles & A. Nettles (Eds.), *Equity and excellence in educational testing and assessment* (pp. 69–87). Boston: Kluwer Academic.

Banks, J. A., & Banks, C. A. M. (1993). *Multicultural education: Issues and perspectives* (2nd ed.). Boston: Allyn & Bacon.

Berman, P. (1997). *Studies of education reform: School reform and student diversity.* Washington, DC: U.S. Department of Education.

Berman, P., McLaughlin, B., McLeod, B., Minicucci, C., Nelson, B., & Woodworth, K. (1995). *School reform and student diversity: Case studies of exemplary practices for LEP students.* Washington, DC: National Clearinghouse for Bilingual Education.

Cabello, B. (1984). Cultural interface in reading comprehension: An alternative explanation. *Bilingual Review, 2,* 12–20.

Center for Applied Linguistics. (1998). *Enriching content classes for secondary ESOL students: Student guide.* McHenry, IL: Delta Systems.

Clements, B., Lara, J., & Cheung, O. (1992). *The feasibility of collecting comparable national statistics about students with limited proficiency.* Washington, DC: Council of Chief State School Officers.

Collier, V. P. (1987). Age and rate of acquisition for academic purposes. *TESOL Quarterly, 21,* 617–641.

Collier, V. P. (1995). Acquiring a second language for school. *Directions in Language and Education, 1*(4), 1–12. Washington, DC: National Clearinghouse for English Language Acquisition and Language Instruction Educational Programs.

Collier, V. P., & Thomas, W. P. (1997). *School effectiveness for language minority students.* Washington, DC: National Clearinghouse for English Language Acquisition and Language Instruction Educational Programs.

Corcoran, T., & Goertz, M. (1995). Instructional capacity and higher performance schools. *Educational Researcher, 24*(9), 27–31.

Council for Basic Education. (1998). *Great expectations: Defining and assessing the rigor in state standards for mathematics and English language arts.* Washington, DC: Author.

Darling-Hammond, L. (1994). Performance-based assessment and educational equity. *Harvard Educational Review, 64*(1), 5–30.

Darling-Hammond, L. (1997). *The right to learn: A blueprint for creating schools that work.* San Francisco: Jossey-Bass.

Darling-Hammond, L. (1998, August). Alternatives to grade retention. *The School Administrator, 55*(7), 18–21.

Darling-Hammond, L., & Loewenberg-Ball, D. (1998). *Teaching for high standards: What policymakers need to know and be able to do.* Philadelphia: CPRE.

Darling-Hammond, L., & Sykes, G. (1999). *Teaching as the learning profession: Handbook of policy and practice.* San Francisco: Jossey-Bass.

Estrin, E. T. (1993). Alternative assessment: Issues in language, culture, and equity. *Far West Laboratory Knowledge Brief No. 11.* San Francisco: Far West Laboratory.

Estrin, E., & Nelson-Barber, S. (1995). Issues in cross-cultural assessment: American Indian and Alaska Native students. *Far West Laboratory Knowledge Brief No. 12.* San Francisco: Far West Laboratory.

Farr, B., & Trumbull, E. (1997). *Assessment alternatives for diverse classrooms.* Norwood, MA: Christopher-Gordon.

FairTest: The National Center for Fair & Open Testing. (2000). *Bilingual Assessment Fact Sheet.* Cambridge, MA: Author.

Fillmore, L. W. (1999, February). *The class of 2002: Will everybody be there?* Paper presented at the Alaska State Department of Education, Anchorage.

Fillmore, L. W., & Snow, C. E. (2000). *What teachers need to know about language.* Washington, DC: U.S. Department of Education, Office of Educational Research and Improvement.

Finn, C., & Petrelli, M. (Eds.). (2000). *The state of state standards.* Washington, DC: Thomas B. Fordham Foundation.

Garcia, G. (2000). Lessons from research: What is the length of time it takes limited English proficient students to acquire English and succeed in an all-English classroom? *Issue & Brief No. 5.* Washington, DC: National Clearinghouse for Bilingual Education.

Garcia, G. E. (1998). Bilingual children's reading. In M. Kamil, P. Mosenthal, P. D. Pearson, and R. Barr (Eds.), *Handbook of reading research, Vol. 3* Mahwah, NJ: Erlbaum.

Garcia, G., & Pearson, P. (1994). Assessment and diversity. In L. Darling-Hammond (Ed.), *Review of Research in Education, 20* (pp. 337–391). Washington, DC: American Education Research Association.

Gardner, H. (1993). *Frames of mind. The theory of multiple intelligences.* New York: Basic Books.

Goertz, M. E., & Duffy, M. C. (2001, March). Assessment and accountability systems in the 50 states: 1999–2000. *CPRE Research Report*

Series RR-046. Consortium for Policy Research in Education, University of Pennsylvania, Graduate School of Education.

Gordon, E. W. (1992). Implications of diversity in human characteristics for authentic assessment. *CES Technical Report 341.* Los Angeles: University of California, National Center for Research on Evaluation, Standards, and Student Testing (CRESST).

Hernandez, R. (1994). Reducing bias in the assessment of culturally and linguistically diverse populations. *Journal of Educational Issues of Language Minority Students, 14,* 269.

Heubert, J., & Hauser, R. (1999). *High stakes. Testing for tracking, promotion, and graduation.* Washington, DC: National Academy Press.

Hodgkinson, H. (2000). *Educational demographics: What teachers should know.* Alexandria, VA: Association for Supervision and Curriculum Development.

Holmes, D., & Duron, S. (2000). LEP students and high stakes assessment. *Issues concerning LEP students and high stakes assessment.* Washington, DC: National Clearinghouse for Bilingual Education.

Holmes, D., Hedlund, P., & Nickerson, B. (2000). *Accommodating English language learners in state and local assessments.* Washington, DC: National Clearinghouse for Bilingual Education.

Irvine, J. J., & York, D. E. (1995). Learning styles and culturally diverse students: A literature review. In J. Banks & C. Banks (Eds.), *Handbook of research on multicultural education* (pp. 484–497). Boston: Allyn & Bacon.

Kendall, J. S., & Marzano, R. J. (2000). *What works in schools: Translating research into action.* Alexandria, VA: Association for Supervision and Curriculum Development.

Kindler, A. L. (2002). *Survey of the states' limited English proficient students and available education programs and services.* 2000–2001 Summary Report. Washington, DC: National Clearinghouse for English Language Acquisition and Language Instruction Educational Programs.

Koelsch, N., Estrin, E., & Farr, B. (1995). *Guide to developing equitable performance assessments.* San Francisco: WestEd.

Kopriva, R. (2000). *Ensuring accuracy in testing for English language learners.* Washington, DC: Council of Chief State School Officers.

LaCelle-Peterson, M., & Rivera, C. (1994). Is it real for all kids? A framework for equitable assessment policies for English language learners. *Harvard Educational Review, 64*(1), 55–75.

Lachat, M. A. (1994). *High standards for all students: Opportunities and challenges.* South Hampton, NH: Center for Resource Management.

Lachat, M. A. (1999a). *Standards, equity, and cultural diversity.* Providence, RI: Northeast and Islands Regional Educational Laboratory at Brown University.

Lachat, M. A. (1999b). *What policymakers and school administrators need to know about assessment reform and English language learners.* Providence, RI: Northeast and Islands Regional Educational Laboratory at Brown University.

Lachat, M. A., & Williams, M. (1999). Putting student performance data at the center of school reform: New expectations for student achievement and school accountability. In J. DiMartino, J. Clarke, & D. Wolk (Eds.), *Personalized learning: Preparing high school students to create their futures* (pp. 210–228). Lanham, MD: Scarecrow Press.

Lam, T. (1991). Testing of limited English proficient children. In K. E. Green (Ed.), *Educational testing: Issues and applications.* New York: Garland.

Lara, J., & August, D. (1996). *Systemic reform and limited English proficient students.* Washington, DC: Council of Chief State School Officers, and Stanford, CA: Stanford Working Group.

Laturnau, J. (2001). *Standards-based instruction for English language learners.* Honolulu, HI: Pacific Resources for Education and Learning.

Linn, R. (2000). Assessments and accountability. *Education Researcher, 29*(2), 4–16.

Linquanti, R. (1999). *Fostering academic success for English language learners: What do we know?* San Francisco: WestEd.

Madaus, G. F. (1994). A technological and historical consideration of equity issues associated with proposals to change the nation's testing policy. *Harvard Education Review, 1*(64), 76–95.

McDonnell, L. M., & Hill, P. T. (1993). *Newcomers in American schools: Meeting the educational needs of immigrant youth.* Santa Monica, CA: RAND.

McLaughlin, B. (1992). Myths and misconceptions about second language learning: What every teacher needs to unlearn. *Educational Practice Report, No. 5.* Santa Cruz, CA: The National Center for Research on Cultural Diversity and Second Language Learning.

McLaughlin, B., & McLeod, B. (1996, June). *Educating all our children: Improving education for children from culturally and linguistically diverse backgrounds.* Impact Statement/Final Report on the Accomplishments of the National Center for Research on Cultural Diversity and Second Language Learning. Unpublished manuscript.

Meisels, S. J., Dorfman, A., & Steele, D. (1995). Equity and excellence in group-administered and performance-based assessments. In M. Nettles & A. Nettles (Eds.), *Equity and excellence in educational testing and assessment*. Boston: Kluwer Academic.

Meltzer, J. (2001). *Adolescent literacy resources: Linking research and practice*. Providence, RI: Northeast and Islands Regional Education Laboratory at Brown University.

Menken, K. (2000). What are the critical issues in wide-scale assessment of English language learners? In *Framing effective practice: Topics and issues in educating English language learners*. Washington, DC: National Clearinghouse for Bilingual Education.

Menken, K., & Holmes, P. (2000). Standards-based education reform and English language learners. In *Framing effective practice: Topics and issues in educating English language learners*. Washington, DC: National Clearinghouse for Bilingual Education.

Moore, D. W., Bean, T. W., Birdyshaw, D., & Rycik, J. A. (1999). *Adolescent literacy: A position statement for the Commission on Adolescent Literacy of the International Reading Association*. Newark, DE: International Reading Association.

National Center on Accessing the General Curriculum. (2001). *Limited English proficient students and special education*. Wakefield, MA: CAST.

National Clearinghouse for Bilingual Education. (1997). *High stakes assessment: A research agenda for English language learners. Symposium summary*. Washington, DC: Author.

National Reading Panel. (2000). *Teaching children to read: An evidence-based assessment of the scientific research literature on reading and its implications for reading instruction*. Washington, DC: National Institute of Child Health and Human Development.

Neill, M. (1995). Some prerequisites for the establishment of equitable, inclusive multicultural assessment systems. In M. Nettles & A. Nettles (Eds.), *Equity and excellence in educational testing and assessment* (pp. 115–157). Boston: Kluwer Academic.

Newmann, F. M., King, M. B., & Rigdon, M. (1997). Accountability and school performance: Implications from restructuring schools. *Harvard Educational Review, 1*(67), pp. 41–74.

No Child Left Behind Act of 2001, Public Law 107–110, Part A—English Language Acquisition, Language Enhancement, and Academic Achievement Act, Sec. 3102. Purposes. (January 8, 2002) [Online]. Available: *www.ed.gov/policy/elsec/leg/esea02/107-110.pdf*

Northeast and Islands Regional Laboratory at Brown University. (2002). The Diversity Kit: An Introductory Resource for Social Change in Education [Online]. Available: *www.lab.brown.edu/tdl/diversitykit*

Olson, J., & Goldstein, A. (1997). *The inclusion of students with disabilities and limited English proficient students in large-scale assessments: A summary of recent progress.* Washington, DC: National Center for Education Statistics.

Pellegrino, J. P., Chudowsky, N., & Glaser, R. (Eds.). (2001). *Knowing what students know: The science and design of educational assessment.* Washington, DC: National Academy Press.

Ravitch, D. (1995). *National standards in American education: A citizen's guide.* Washington, DC: Brookings Institution Press.

Riddle, W. (1999, October). Education for the disadvantaged: ESEA Title 1 reauthorization issues. *Congressional Research Service Issue Brief.* Washington, DC: The Library of Congress.

Rivera, C. (2000). *State policy for the inclusion and accommodation of ELL in state assessment programs during 1998–1999.* Washington, DC: The George Washington University, Center for Equity and Excellence in Education.

Rivera, C., & Stansfield, C. (1998). Leveling the playing field for English language learners: Increasing participation in state and local assessments through accommodations. In R. Brandt (Ed.), *Assessing student learning: New rules, new realities.* Arlington, VA: Education Research Service.

Rivera, C., & Stansfield, C. (2000). *State policies for the inclusion and accommodation of English language learners in state assessment programs during 1998–1999. Executive Summary.* Washington, DC: The George Washington University, Center for Equity and Excellence in Education.

Rivera, C., & Vincent, C. (1996, June). *High school graduation testing: Policies and practices in the assessment of limited English proficient students.* Paper presented at annual meeting of the National Conference on Large-Scale Assessment, 1996, Phoenix, AZ.

Rivera, C., & Vincent, C. (1997). *High school graduation testing: Policies and practices in the assessment of English language learners.* Washington, DC: Center for Equity and Excellence in Education, The George Washington University, Graduate School of Education and Human Development.

Ruiz de Velasco, J. R., & Fix, M. (2000). Limited English proficient students and high-stakes accountability systems. Rights at risk: Equality in an age of terrorism (Chapter 17, Part Two: Discriminatory Practices in Education.) *7th Biennial Report.* Washington, DC: Citizens' Commission on Civil Rights.

Taylor, C. (1994). Assessment for measurement or standards: The peril and promise of large-scale assessment reform. *American Education Research Journal, 31,* 231–262.

Teachers of English to Speakers of Other Languages. (1997). *ESL standards for pre-K-12 students.* Bloomington, IL: Author.

Teemant, A., Bernhardt, E. B., Rodriquez-Munoz, M., & Aiello, M. (2000, November). A dialogue among teachers that benefits second language learners. Beyond structural change: Effective practices in the middle grades. *Middle School Journal, 32*(2), 26–38.

Thomas, W. P., & Collier, V. P. (2002). *A national study of school effectiveness for language minority students' long-term academic achievement.* Washington, DC: CREDE.

Trail, K. (2000, December). A changing nation: The impact of linguistic and cultural diversity on education. Diversity in Our Schools: New Opportunities for Teaching and Learning. In Southwest Educational Development Laboratory's *SEDL Letter, 12*(2).

U.S. Department of Education annual "Survey of the States' Limited English Proficient Students and Available Programs and Services," 1991–1992 and 2001–2002. U.S. Department of Education, Office for Civil Rights. (1998). Elementary and Secondary School Civil Rights Compliance. [Online]. Available: *www.ed.gov/about/offices/list/ocr/ocrarc.pdf*

Wiggins, G. (1989). Teaching to the (authentic) test. *Educational Leadership, 46,* 41–47.

Williams, B. (Ed.). (1996). *Closing the achievement gap: A vision for changing beliefs and practices.* Alexandria, VA: Association for Supervision and Curriculum Development.

Winfield, L. (1995). Performance-based assessments: Contributor or detractor to equity? In M. Nettles & A. Nettles (Eds.), *Equity and excellence in educational testing and assessment,* (pp. 221–241). Boston: Kluwer Academic.

Wolf, D., Bixby, J., Glenn, J., & Gardner, H. (1991). To use their minds well: Investigating new forms of student assessment. In G. Grant (Ed.), *Review of research in education.* Washington, DC: American Educational Research Association.

Wolf, D. P., LeMahieu, P. G., & Eresch, J. A. (1992). Good measure: Assessment as a tool for educational reform. *Educational Leadership, 49,* 8–13.

Zehler, A. (1994, Summer). Working with English language learners: Strategies for elementary and middle school teachers. *NCBE Program Information Guide Series, No. 10.*

Index

**CORWIN
PRESS**

The Corwin Press logo—a raven striding across an open book—represents the union of courage and learning. Corwin Press is committed to improving education for all learners by publishing books and other professional development resources for those serving the field of K–12 education. By providing practical, hands-on materials, Corwin Press continues to carry out the promise of its motto: **"Helping Educators Do Their Work Better."**